How To Make

A Pastor's Wife

Dear Geri,

I hope you enjoy reading this as much as I enjoyed writing it.

God Bless,

Katrina xx

How To Make

A Pastor's Wife

Katrina Cracknell

Published by Withyland Heights Publishing
Kilcot, Newent, Glos. UK

HOW TO MAKE A PASTOR'S WIFE

ISBN 978-0-9553051-3-9

Book formatted by www.bookformatting.co.uk.

Contents

Introduction 1
Chapter One 3
Chapter Two 10
Chapter Three 19
Chapter Four 29
Chapter Five 35
Chapter Six 42
Chapter Seven 49
Chapter Eight 59
Chapter Nine 67
Chapter Ten 76
Chapter Eleven 82
Chapter Twelve 89
Chapter Thirteen 97
Chapter Fourteen 107
Chapter Fifteen 114
About the Author 120

“Katrina has written a heart moving, yet very real story of her journey of faith. It is a tale which will delight, amuse and tear your heart strings as she describes the joys and pain of shared ministry with her pastor/farmer husband Tim. They are a lovable couple with whom we were delighted to share ministry with at The Garden Tomb and get to know them better.”

Rosalind Meryon – Author of “A Garden in Jerusalem”.

“Katrina has a wonderful talent for creating vivid descriptions of people she has known and who have influenced her. In this book she brings insights and understanding of people with depth and compassion, as well as sharing her own journey with an honesty that is sometimes raw in its vulnerability. Her stories and insights are deeply moving in places, hilarious in others, and the addition of her own poems add significantly to the emotional impact of the book. I loved reading it, especially the way she draws our attention to our wonderful God throughout. I think it will be really helpful for our young people (and older people) to read, as it's a great lesson in not dismissing ourselves from serving God.”

Fiona Taylor - Professional musician, Worship Leader, author of "The Worshipping Musician".

For my husband Tim who has journeyed with me on this roller-coaster ride of discovering God's plan and purpose for our lives. It hasn't been easy, but your loving support and gentle encouragement have bolstered me when I needed it and carried me through the storms. Thank you.

Acknowledgements

My thanks to the many people who encouraged me and supported me in the writing of this book, those who gave me permission to write about loved ones who are no longer with us and those who proof-read my finished work and gave me helpful feedback and advice. To all who cheered me on in this endeavour and who and helped me believe in myself – thank you.

Introduction

I have always loved writing.

I love writing poems, prose, letters, notes and e-mails and for the last ten years or more I have journaled most days. I have a drawer full of journals filled with my thoughts, struggles, questions, achievements and conversations with God. Writing is my therapy - my way of processing the complexities of life and the plethora of emotions that everyday events evoke.

Recently, after reading a book written by a fellow pastor's wife, I found myself wondering how I might approach writing a book describing my journey to the place I find myself in today. How does God make a pastor's wife? Would every pastor's wife be made up of the same ingredients? I doubt it. The Bible tells us we are all one-of-a-kind masterpieces, unique and wonderfully made - our personalities, abilities and life experiences are very different just as rock cakes and chocolate brownies look and taste nothing alike and yet are both cakes! At the breakfast table one morning I voiced my thoughts to my husband Tim and remarked that if I were to write a book about being a pastor's wife it would be grounded in simple stories rather than deep theological teaching. Tim's matter-of-fact response was, "Jesus used stories all the time. "

That statement kept resonating in my head and was the seed for this book.

I very much enjoyed reading William Zinsser's book, "Writing about your life " in which he drops pearls of wisdom into the would-be-writer's lap. I took to heart his sound advice when he writes:

"Don't visualize the finished product at the end of your journey;

it will look different when you get there. Be ready to be surprised by the crazy, wonderful events that will come dancing out of your past when you stir the pot of memory. Embrace those long-lost visitors. If they shove aside some events you originally thought you wanted to write about, it's because they have more vitality. Go with what interests and amuses you. Trust the process, and the product will take care of itself. "

I am aware that in the following pages there are many people whose lives have intertwined with mine and who I have not mentioned - had I included them all this book would be a much thicker tome. This in no way undermines their importance in my life's journey but it was simply a case of having to be selective about specific incidents which I hoped would engage with the reader.

The following chapters are not full of deep Biblical teaching. I am not a theologian. I have not been to Bible School. I feel ill equipped for my role as a pastor's wife but I have come to accept that in his wisdom this is the role God has given me and he knows best. I have tried to give an insight into who I am by using stories of the events in my life that brought me to this point and I have attempted to be honest and real with the struggles along the way. I have made mistakes and I will continue to make mistakes - that's simply part of my humanness. William Zinsser observes: "To write well about your life you only have to be true to yourself. If you make an honest transaction with your remembered experiences and emotions you'll reach the readers you want to reach. "

I have striven to be true to myself and if this book encourages you in any small way as you follow your life's path, then it has been worth the writing.

Chapter One

Proverbs 22:6 (NLT)
Direct your children onto the right path,
and when they are older, they will not leave it.

Early Influences

During my training as a primary school teacher I can remember one lecture in which a famous child psychologist was quoted as saying, "Give me a child until he is seven and I will give you the man ". If I'm honest that is pretty much all I remember about my four years of study for my B.Ed. degree but then those that know me, know how appalling my memory is! The point is, it's those early years that are the most informative and which play a large part in a child's development in all sorts of ways.

When my parents first married in December 1965, Dad was in the Merchant Navy and so was away from home for long periods of time. As a consequence, Mum continued to live with her parents on a small farm on the outskirts of Hereford until I was four years old. My grandparents, Roby and Eva, were churchgoers and attended the local Anglican Church in the nearby village of Much Dewchurch where my parents were married, where my sister and I were christened and where later I would marry my husband Tim.

Grandad was a sidesperson and was responsible for giving out hymn books, greeting people as they came through the door and taking up the collection. As a child I can remember him taking me to church with him on Sunday mornings and sitting in the pew watching him carry out his various duties with a quiet reverence.

My grandad was a strong, lean man with big hands that were used to manual labour and yet he had a gentle and unassuming manner which drew people to him. There was nothing showy or flamboyant about him but he was a steady influence in my life and I remember at his funeral the vicar described him as a man who knew what it was to be content. Certainly, that was my experience of him. He loved his family, he loved his garden, he loved his cows (he had 2 or 3 cows that he milked by hand) and he loved his work outside in the apple orchards. Looking back, I see now that he loved his God too but his faith wasn't something he ever talked about to me, it was a private thing between him and God but I caught glimpses of it as I watched him on a Sunday morning and as he went about his daily life enjoying nature and communing with the Creator. I am grateful for the way he shaped those early years and I tried to capture those memories in the following poem written after his death at the age of 92.

MEMORIES OF GRANDAD
As I lie here alone in the dark of the night
Wishing you onward in your heavenward flight,
My mind wanders back over the decades of time
And memories of you flash into my mind.
As a small girl it was my early morning treat
To watch you milk the cows on your three-legged seat,
As the stream of frothy milk hit the metal pail
Stray cats around your feet kept up a hungry wail.
Then donning your hat, off to work you would go
Your bait in a bag and at your side old Carlo,
To supervise the pickers, to prune and to spray
Before coming home tired at the end of the day.
To be first down the stairs was your morning routine,
To stoke up the Rayburn and brew up the tea.
I liked watching you shave at the sink in your vest,
With the bryll cream slapped on you'd pass any test!
On Sundays off to church we would go at half nine
Parking the car as the bells began to chime,

Giving out the hymn books as the people drifted in
And standing beside you, we'd all start to sing.
Feeling so proud as you followed me up the aisle
Greeting all your friends with a nod and a smile,
Your big hands took the bread as we knelt reverently
Whilst the crimson-clad choir sang hymns quietly.
Often when I came down the garden you'd be found
Planting bulbs and seeds and digging in the ground,
Picking ripe tomatoes in the greenhouse for tea
The riot of colour was quite a sight to see!
So farewell gentle grandad, I bid you goodbye,
May angels escort you as heavenwards you fly;
As you shake off this world's shackles and rise above
Our memories of you will be coloured with love.

My grandmother used to sing in the church choir and I can remember craning my neck from the pew at the back of the church to catch a glimpse of her as the choir entered from the vestry in their red cassocks and white surplices. Then, when grandad took me up to the Communion rail, I would sneak a look at her as she sang and she would give me a smile. At home, Nan would be responsible for looking after me while mum went out to work as a hairdresser. I would often play under the table in the farmhouse kitchen while Nan taught me songs like "Jesus loves me this I know ", and "Jesus wants me as a sunbeam ", to name but a couple. Once again, Nan never shared her faith with me but she loved to sing hymns and so from an early age I was aware of God through simple Bible stories and songs and I was able to witness first-hand the importance of my grandparents' faith. When my Nan was in hospital towards the end of her life, I remember singing hymns to her as she dozed and telling her it was OK for her to let go of life. On one occasion she was quite definite that she could see them "waiting for her " and when I quizzed her on who she could see she told me it was grandad and her mother and father. I have no doubts that they are all now reunited in a far better place. They may not have verbalised their faith in the way I might do but they were part of my spiritual journey and I want to recognise them for the important part they played.

When I was four my Dad got a job as an engineer with the cross-channel ferry company, Townsend Thoresen, and we moved to the south of England to a village called St. Margaret's-at-Cliff in Kent. I started school not long after and my sister Michelle was born. Sadly I don't remember much of my childhood at this time but then when I was nine we moved again to another village called Shepherdswell where I attended the local Church of England school. The vicar, Reverend Hugh Mansfield-Williams, used to come in to school regularly to take RE lessons. He was a round, bald-headed man who simply didn't have a clue how to connect with children and as a result mayhem would ensue each time he turned his back to write on the blackboard as missiles were fired across the room by the more challenging members of the class. He never could work out who was responsible and would just get more red-faced and almost apoplectic.

Mum sent my sister and I to the weekly Sunday School and from this I progressed to joining the church choir, following in my Nan’s footsteps. I too got to wear a red cassock, white serplice and ruff and felt very important in my chorister's uniform. The vicar's sermons were no more inspiring than his RE lessons so I can't say I got any spiritual nourishment from them but I loved to sit in the choir stalls and take in the pictures on the stained glass windows, the crucifix hanging on the wall and the quiet peacefulness of the cool, dim interior. I loved the rhythm of the service, the prayers and responses, the psalms and the hymns and the encouraging smiles from the congregation.

At about this time a lovely older couple called Mr & Mrs Taylor took an interest in my spiritual development along with my sister and few other young people. They invited us to their home after the church service which they attended. They would give us a drink and a biscuit and then would have prepared some Sunday School material for us to have a look at. Again, I don't remember the details of these lessons but I do remember their kind, gentle encouragement as they sought to teach us Bible truths. Several years ago I managed to track them down and sent them a card to thank them for their godly influence on my journey of faith and they seemed thrilled to hear from me. Mary Taylor has since died but I am still in regular contact with her husband, John, and he receives our newsletters.

Another influence in my life around this time was the move from a small village primary school to the large Girls' Grammar School in Dover. I had done well when taking the Kent Test which meant that I was offered a sought-after place at the local grammar school much to my parents' delight. However, after having been a big fish in a little pond I found the transition to the ocean rather overwhelming and felt out of my depth well and truly! My particular problem was with the maths teacher, Miss Johnson. She was the sort of teacher who expected to explain something only once (because after all we were in the top set!) and woe betide you if you needed further coaching. Unfortunately for me, I did. I struggled with grasping new mathematical concepts and it was all gobbledygook to me. Not wanting to incur her wrath or disdain I kept quiet, kept my head down and felt a rising panic engulf me as each maths lesson loomed. My homework was a complete mystery - she might just as well have placed Egyptian hieroglyphics in front of me for all the sense it made. My dad, who is good with numbers, tried to coach me but this only made matters worse. Methods of teaching had changed since he was at school and when he tried to teach me his way of approaching the problem it simply confused me more and I often ended up in tears while he was totally exasperated with me. We laugh about it now and he still maintains he's a patient man (mum begs to differ), but at the time I found the whole thing very traumatic. It was a vicious circle. I felt a failure and thought I was going to get ousted from the grammar school I had worked so hard to get into thereby letting my parents down. This meant I wasn't sleeping at night which in turn made me tired and unable to concentrate on my lessons during the day which further exacerbated the situation. It looked hopeless but God came to the rescue in the form of the Gideons. One day during that first school term two visitors from The Gideon Society came to explain their work in our morning assembly and at the end they offered each girl a small New

Testament Bible. I took mine and listened as they explained how there was a section in the front which told you where you could find help when certain circumstances assailed you.

That night when I went to bed, I turned to the front section of my Gideon New Testament and found "worry " listed and alongside it the corresponding reference for Matthew 6: 25-34. Those verses became a life-saver for me. I read them through several times before settling down for the night and had the best night's sleep in months. I woke feeling refreshed and somehow different. God had spoken to me through those verses in His word and each night thereafter I would read them and sense God's soothing presence. It wasn't long before things started to improve at school. I wasn't as tired and so could concentrate better in class. Slowly the penny dropped and the concepts I had been grappling with finally made sense like a veil being lifted from my eyes. All this because two unknown Gideon members took the time to give a New Testament to a young girl who so desperately needed to hear God's voice saying, "Do not worry! " and who would embark on a journey that would last the rest of her life.

A big change took place when a new vicar replaced Reverend Hugh Mansfield-Williams in the parish of Shepherdswell. The new incumbent was a retired headmaster of the Boys' Grammar School in Dover and his background in teaching and education meant he was well suited to connect with a young girl like me. Father Michael Hinton was like a breath of fresh air. He and his lovely wife, Jean, opened the vicarage to the few young people connected to the church and he started a Sunday evening discipleship group called "Quest ". I used to love going along each week with a couple of my friends and I remember on one occasion we fasted and camped out overnight on the village green to raise money for some good cause. Father Michael was full of energy and great ideas. He challenged our thinking and gave us a greater Biblical understanding. I can recall one Sunday evening when he took us through the rituals of an authentic Jewish Passover meal step by step, explaining the significance of each item eaten. He would encourage debate and discussion and would raise our awareness of world issues and how we could strive to make a difference. When considering the people who influenced my life in terms of spiritual growth, Father Michael was a major player and we still keep in touch via e-mails occasionally.

So God played a quiet but consistent role through my childhood and early teenage years and I'm sure he was responsible for putting in place people who would pray for me through the more turbulent years which were ahead. I am grateful to these men and women of God who gave their time and energy in obedience to the call of God on their lives and I sincerely hope I can emulate them by pouring myself into the lives of others.

Chapter Two

Proverbs 17:17 (NIV)
A friend loves at all times, and a brother is born for a time of adversity.

Optima Tenete

For the most part I enjoyed my days at secondary school. Dover Grammar School for Girls was founded in 1910 and the school motto which was emblazoned on our blazer badge when we embarked on our secondary education in September 1978 was 'Optima Tenete' which means 'hold on to the best'. That's about the only Latin I can remember from two years of studying the language!

I had to catch the train from our little village of Shepherdswell to Dover where the grammar school was situated and on that very first morning I was feeling a little anxious about the whole new routine. As I stood on the platform in my pristine uniform I remember seeing a blonde-haired girl crossing the footbridge dressed in identical navy Girls Grammar School uniform. Little did I know then that we would become best friends for the rest of our school days.

Catherine had attended a Catholic primary school in Canterbury and although we lived in the same village, our paths had never crossed until that moment in time. She was one of five children and her home was to become my second home as I would spend a huge amount of time there and I also became good friends with her sister Claire who was just a year younger than us. Catherine was a fun-loving character with a charismatic personality which drew people to her. We soon became good friends, meeting on the platform each morning, sitting together on the train and walking the mile or so to school once we arrived in Dover. I felt privileged to be part of Catherine's "gang " as she was out-going, sporty and always at the centre of everything - quite the opposite of me! Our birthdays were only 3 days apart and the fact she went to Catholic Mass each week gave us a church connection which was part of the strong bond we shared.

Catherine was always looking for opportunities to play the joker and would do the most outrageous things. Once as I was stood minding my own business on the station platform one morning I looked across to the opposite platform to see Catherine staggering up the steps wearing a vivid blue afro wig and the highest pair of platform shoes I had ever seen. She could hardly walk in the shoes and was in constant danger of falling off them and breaking her ankles. She got some astonished looks from other commuters on the platform but kept a completely straight face as she teetered up to me and stood waiting for the train as if this was her usual attire. I can't remember now what had sparked off this radical new look but she walked some of the way to school in the ridiculous shoes until her poor feet could stand the pain no longer. Now you need to bear in mind that the protocol for our school uniform was very strict and so a bright blue afro wig was somewhat conspicuous. Our first lesson of the day was geography and our teacher Mrs Pennington was a diminutive lady with a loud voice. When her eyes were drawn to the mop of blue hair on Catherine's head, she asked Catherine quite firmly to remove the wig at which point Catherine's amateur dramatics began. Her face crumpled and she hid her head in her arms on her desk as she pretended to sob hysterically whilst explaining that in trying to dye her hair the previous evening it had all gone horribly wrong and now she was now a laughing stock! Poor Mrs Pennington was completely taken in. She apologised to the still distraught pupil and told her not to worry - it would all work out OK and she carried on the lesson without a further reference to Catherine's blue hair! I can only presume she explained the situation to the rest of the staff in the staffroom later as Catherine continued to wear the wig for the rest of the day unchallenged. The next day the wig had disappeared and her coiffure was back to normal so I have no idea what the teaching staff made of it all - presumably they assumed she had visited a hairdresser to rectify the mistake!

Catherine was full of pranks which used to make us all laugh but I used to get very hot under the collar fearing she would get found out. Another time she had the whole French class and the teacher, Madame Riley, on their hands and knees on the floor of the language lab looking for fictitious contact lenses! She always managed to hold her nerve and keep a straight face and I was always too scared to snigger or smile. Catherine had a powerful singing voice and our music teacher Mrs Dunn often used to try and persuade her to have her voice trained. Every morning the whole school would file into assembly one form at a time and sit cross-legged on the floor. We would sing a couple of hymns, have a little thought for the day, listen to notices and say a prayer or two before filing back out and going to our first lesson. During the hymns Catherine would deliberately hold on a note for longer or come in a couple of notes early at the beginning of a verse and as usual keep a dead straight face whilst the rest of the school were trying hard not to dissolve into fits of giggles and give the game away. I'm sure the teachers guessed she was doing it deliberately but she was such a good actress that they couldn't prove anything so she was never reprimanded. In fact, on one occasion, some of the younger members of the school were kept behind after assembly and got a severe telling off by one of the teachers for laughing at Catherine’s singing while she seemed apparently oblivious to the hilarity it was causing. It certainly livened up what were otherwise deadly assemblies.

However, I distinctly remember one assembly when things went too far even by Catherine's standards. It was when we were in the third year at school (the equivalent of Year 9 today) and we were having registration with our form teacher before filing into the assembly hall. Catherine was obviously feeling bored and so announced to a few of us that she was planning on fainting in assembly that day. I tried to dissuade her but her mind was made up and so I resigned myself to the fact that there was likely to be a bit of drama that morning. We filed in as usual and sat cross-legged for the first part of the assembly in which I silently prayed that she would change her mind but we then stood up to sing the first hymn and it wasn't long before I heard Catherine breathing heavily beside me. I gave her a nudge which she ignored and the laboured breathing continued as other people around us started to look at her strangely. Suddenly her legs buckled and she crumpled to the floor with a loud thud and lay motionless. It was all action stations. As the students around her looked on with stunned faces, two members of staff rushed along the row, grabbed Catherine's arms and dragged her along the row and out through the double doors at the front of the hall. Those of us "in the know " couldn't believe she had actually gone through with it but it wasn't over yet. As we filed out of the assembly hall on our way to lessons we passed Catherine still lying motionless in the hallway with several staff fussing anxiously over her whilst trying to elevate her feet above her head. I silently willed her to open her eyes and stop the prank right now as it had gone far enough.

We all went to lessons and half expected to see Catherine walk through the door but when there had been no sign of her by lunch time we asked our form teacher how she was and were horrified to hear she had been taken to hospital and her parents had been called! The rest of the day passed in a haze of disbelief that a prank could have gone so terribly wrong. When Catherine arrived on the station platform the following morning looking somewhat sheepish I discovered that she had done such a convincing act of fainting that she had believed it herself and had been horrified to find herself in a hospital bed with a white-coated doctor hovering over her. Needless to say she didn't try that one again and we were sworn to secrecy because if her poor parents ever found out it had all started out as a joke, she would have been in more than a little hot water!

The headmistress of the Grammar School was a force to be reckoned with. Her name was Miss Hasler and she would patrol the narrow corridors of the school wearing her black and red robes like a giant bird of prey. She would suck air in through the sides of her mouth with a hissing sound when something didn't please her and would fix her dark, beady eyes on you and pin you to the spot. Everyone had a healthy respect for her and you certainly didn't want to be called to her office for a misdemeanour. She taught history and I suspect that having her as my history teacher in the fifth year is what put me off the subject as on one occasion she caught me talking in class and my punishment was to give a two minute speech on a subject of her choosing at the beginning of the next lesson.

In the sixth form Catherine was elected deputy head girl, a much sought-after accolade, and one which reflected her popularity. She and the head girl had seats of prominence on the stage in the assembly hall along with twelve prefects (of which I was one) and she wore her badge proudly pinned to her uniform. Sometime after this, due to some misdemeanour that I can't recall, Catherine was called to Miss Hasler's office and made to stand in front of the headmistress's desk while she was interrogated. She had foolishly mentioned her forthcoming ordeal to Jo Chandler, one of our group of friends, who thought it would be a good idea to hide under the headmistress's office window. As Catherine was stood facing the window getting hauled over the coals, all she could see was our friend Jo's face bobbing up and down outside the window which of course made her laugh. This did nothing to appease the formidable Miss Hasler who was completely incensed by her seeming disregard for authority and Catherine's punishment was to have her Deputy Head Girl badge taken from her. She was devastated. Thankfully, sometime later, she was reinstated to her former position but it was no doubt a steep learning curve for her and taught her she couldn't always get away with everything!

My favourite subject at school was English and in the fourth year we were taught by the deputy head teacher, Mrs. Evans, who was of Welsh origin. On one occasion I can remember she was late arriving for our lesson and so it gave us time for some high jinks.

Firstly, we sprinkled some drawing pins on her chair and then tucked it back under the desk at the front of the classroom. Then, for some reason, we thought it would be fun to throw someone's shoes out of the window. I think it was either Catherine's or Jo's shoes that got thrown around the room and then dropped out of the big sash windows onto the grass surround at the front of the school. The Grammar School was an imposing five storey brick building and so it took a couple of minutes for the owner of the shoes to run down the several staircases and outside to retrieve the shoes. As the rest of the class hung out of the window to watch the proceedings, the school caretaker appeared around the corner, saw the shoes on the grass, picked them up and walked off with them. By the time the owner of the shoes arrived at the scene after negotiating several flights of stairs, the shoes had mysteriously disappeared and they were left standing bare-footed wondering what could possibly have happened to them. When Mrs. Evans finally arrived for the lesson, the shoeless person had their feet tucked under their desk in the hope she wouldn't notice and we all waited with baited breath as she walked to the front, pulled out her chair and sat down. Instead of the anticipated yelp of pain and a sudden springing to her feet, there was absolutely no response. She conducted the lesson from her seat at the front as usual and then at the end stood and walked out with no indication she had been suffering any discomfort from the drawing pins adorning her chair much to our disappointment!

Whilst not actually directly to do with school but nonetheless resulting from a friendship formed at school, was our holiday to Butlin's at Bognor Regis. Cindy was a girl in the year above us who shared Catherine's love of sport and they played on the school teams alongside each other. Just after Cindy's eighteenth birthday, when Catherine and I were both seventeen and her sister Claire was sixteen, the four of us decided to go on holiday to Butlin's. As Cindy was technically an adult now, (a dubious title!) she was able to take responsibility for us all and so we booked a chalet for a week and set our sights on the bright lights of Bognor Regis. We had a brilliant week. Everything was included in the package so we had full use of the leisure facilities and fairground rides and in the evenings we enjoyed the discos and cabarets. Most days would find us in the swimming pool where I developed a school-girl crush on one of the Redcoat lifeguards called Eddie. On one occasion I was both flattered and mortified when he blew his whistle so that everyone in the swimming pool stopped and then in the expectant silence he pointed at me and shouted, "You! " followed by a more melodic, "are the sunshine of my life ". I still have a signed photo of the four of us with Eddie the Redcoat as a memento of our time at Butlin's and can never hear that song without thinking of being serenaded by him.

Another memory I have is of the Golden Grill restaurant. I recall that we cooked most of our meals in the chalet accommodation but on one evening the four of us got all dressed up and booked a table at one of the restaurants on site – The Golden Grill. I have no idea what struck us as funny but at one point near the end of the meal we started laughing about something and just couldn't stop. We laughed so hard that Cindy suddenly gasped, leapt from the table and ran out of the door. When we looked down at her chair we realised all the laughing had caused her to have an accident and wet herself which of course then started Catherine and Claire off into more convulsions of mirth as they headed for the door in hot pursuit leaving me to pull myself together sufficiently to be able to pay the bill and try and allay the restaurant staff's fears that I wasn't about to do a runner like the other three! We never let Cindy forget that evening. As the "adult " of the party she had been the one to cause total disarray and just the mention of the name "Golden Grill " was enough to send us into fits of giggles from that day onwards.

Catherine, Jo and I all stayed on into the sixth form and sat our 'A' levels and then before we knew it the time had come to say goodbye to the friends we had shared seven years of our lives with. It was a sad time in many ways as I sensed it was a pivotal moment in my life and I tried to capture this in a poem I wrote on the day we left. Jo went on to become a vet, Catherine headed off to study sports at Crewe and I postponed my plans for a year as I didn't get the grades I needed to study Speech Therapy. Our lives took us in different directions and we made new friends and quite quickly grew apart. More recently, with the arrival of Facebook on the scene, I have reconnected a little with Catherine who now lives in Invercargill, New Zealand with her husband and two children and also with Jo who still lives in Kent with her husband and three daughters. Who knows maybe one day we'll have a reunion? I vote the venue is New Zealand!

OPTIMA TENETE (written in 1985)
A gentle sadness prevails;
The certain knowledge that things can never again be what they once were.
Before us is a strange road – narrow and winding and hiding unknown hazards.
Behind us is a golden land – our early childhood and schooldays,
Moments of childlike innocence.
A time of comparatively trivial worries,
A time of discovering who we really are,
Of building bonds of love with those around us.
Now with our newly found identity,
We must take our first tottering steps down the long road.
We must focus our eyes on the distant horizon, not glance longingly over our shoulders
At the land we can never again enter.
Thus the glistening eyes and wet lashes accompany the realisation
That a stage of our lives has slipped
Uncontrollably and irretrievably from our hands.
We have progressed from children to young women
And as such we must now be brave and boldly venture forth
Into this new world and take all it has to offer us
Both good and bad.
Do not scorn us or deny us these last few moments together.
Although unspoken, there is a deep mutual understanding
That despite heart-felt promises, we will never again be quite so close,

> Never again will the feelings generated in these last few moments be rekindled.
> Thus the gentle drops of sorrow signify the end of an era.
> Goodbye my friends and may peace and happiness be with you always.

After leaving school I took a year out to work for a hovercraft company, Hoverspeed, as a telephone reservations assistant in the offices in Dover. To make the best use of this interim time I also signed up to an evening class in typing which has stood me in good stead ever since as I can touch-type – although not very speedily! Then the next exciting phase of my life began with me leaving home to start a four year B.Ed. Honours degree course at Bath College of Higher Education in September 1986. In the August I was presented with a study Bible "in gratitude for many years of faithful service to church and choir " by the parish of St. Andrew, Shepherdswell and then it was time to spread my wings and fly as the bright lights of Bath beckoned to me.

Chapter Three

Jeremiah 29:13 (NIV)
You will seek me and find me when you seek me with all your heart.

Sisters

As I've already mentioned, I have one sister called Michelle who is five years my junior. I don't remember anything about her arrival on the scene but life with her around was certainly not boring. She has always been the stronger personality, the one to push boundaries and make her presence felt and anything she sets her sights on, she attains. Growing up together we didn't always see eye to eye, in fact, there were many times when we wound each other up and just didn't want to be in each other's company. Michelle always appeared fearless and unstoppable. She was the first child to attain the dubious feat of escaping from the Playgroup at the tender age of three by climbing through a hole in the hedge and this Houdini act was not the first or the last!

Because Dad worked on the cross-channel ferries one of the perks of the job was much discounted rates for day trips for family members to France. One hot summer's day while my grandparents were staying with us on holiday and Michelle was about 3 years old, we decided the six of us would spend the day on the beach near Calais and so caught the ferry over to France. The beach was heaving with people but we managed to find a little spot to spread ourselves out and settled down to enjoy the sunshine as Michelle and I changed into swimming costumes. All was well until Mum glanced up and asked, “Where's Michelle? “ In the few moments they had let their attention wander from watching her play with her bucket and spade in the sand next to my Nan, she had gone! We looked up and down the beach among the hundreds of sun worshippers but in that split second it was if she had been spirited away without a trace. Panic ensued. My grandad, dad and mum all went off in different directions to look for her while I stayed with my Nan in case by some miracle she returned. The added complication was the fact that only dad spoke a little French so my mum and grandad had to use gestures to ask people on the beach if they had seen an unaccompanied toddler. For the next fifteen minutes they searched up and down the beach, reporting back regularly to see if there was any news from base where nan and I sat feeling helpless and increasingly alarmed. Nothing. My little sister had just vanished on a foreign beach in a matter of seconds. Amidst all the panic and fear a voice was then heard on a tannoy system across the beach making an urgent announcement in French. Dad managed to make out it was the Police and that it was something about a little girl being found. Mum and dad hurried up the beach to where the announcement was being broadcast from to find Michelle sitting quite happily on a female police officer's knee, not in the least bit phased by her strange surroundings. As soon as she saw my parents she exclaimed, “I tried to find you Mummy but I couldn't! “ Apparently she had been wandering on the beach asking groups of people, “Where my Mummy gone? “ When she got no response (they probably couldn’t understand this English speaking toddler) she had moved on to the next group until some kind person had eventually taken her to the police in an attempt to find her parents. The whole experience whilst traumatising the rest of the family and leaving an indelible mark on our memories, seemed to have no adverse effect on Michelle, who continued to do her Houdini acts at every opportunity.

Early one Saturday morning when Michelle was four, Mum came downstairs to find the back door unlocked and Michelle gone. She had found a 10p coin on the kitchen side, dragged a chair to the back door and unlocked it and then gone to her friend's house whose garden was adjacent to ours. She had knocked at the door and asked the mum if her daughter, also called Michelle, would like to go to the sweet shop with her to buy some sweets. The unwitting parent assumed my Mum was taking them to the shop in the car and so allowed the two four-year olds to go off clutching the 10p piece. Sometime later and much to the neighbour's horror my mum phoned to ask if my sister Michelle was there as she had disappeared from the house before we had got up. It soon became apparent what had happened and so my distraught Mum got in the car to drive the half mile along a busy main road to the sweet shop only to find the two little girls nonchalantly on their way back from their shopping expedition happily clutching a paper bag of sweets between them! Michelle had no idea what all the fuss was about and this was to be her usual response to similar events.

When Michelle was about 3 years old and I was 8, Dad bravely (or foolishly) took us both to the nearby town of Deal to buy a Mother's Day card and present for mum. We went into Woolworth's in the hope of gaining some inspiration and it wasn't long before Michelle had given dad the slip and done her disappearing act. Dad told me to stay put while he went off to try and locate my wayward sister and promised he would come back and get me when he had found her. I dutifully stood where I had been told to wait. Dad scoured the shop floor for some time and eventually noticed a commotion down behind a counter where the shop assistant was stood. He went to investigate and found Michelle sat on the floor at the lady's feet quite happily playing with whatever had caught her attention and totally unaware of the panic she had caused my dad by her absence. He retrieved his errant daughter and then retraced his steps to find me. I hadn't moved from the spot but by the time he found me I was a blubbering wreck as I was convinced he had found my sister, forgotten me and left the shop! I was beside myself thinking I had been abandoned. We still laugh about it now - how could two sisters be so different? Michelle so strong-willed and independent and me so sensitive and lacking in confidence - chalk and cheese.

On another occasion at about the same age I remember going

upstairs to our bedroom to check on Michelle as mum had asked me to. I looked in the bedroom but there was no sign of Michelle then as I passed the door to the guest room I heard a little voice call my name. I walked into the room but it appeared empty. I called her name and heard a faint voice coming through the open window. I climbed up on a table and looked out and there was Michelle sitting on the flat roof of the conservatory below me. She had climbed out of the window, slid down the tiled roof and then been unable to climb back up. I ran down the stairs yelling, "Mum, Michelle has climbed out of the window! " My poor mum was suffering with glandular fever and had a friend visiting her. Mum immediately thought I meant Michelle had climbed out of our bedroom window which has a sheer drop onto a concrete driveway and she imagined the worst! She flew out of the front door and stood looking perplexed when there was no sign of Michelle. Once I had explained it was the guest room window, a rescue attempt was planned. Mum's friend Barbara was a tall, athletic lady and so she wriggled her way out of the bedroom window with Mum holding tightly onto her ankles, stretched down the tiled roof and grabbed my sister's hand and started hauling her back up the roof and in through the window. Mission accomplished - like a cat with nine lives she had survived again!

Being the older sister meant that I was often put in charge of my younger, wayward sibling and whilst part of me enjoyed bossing her around, it wasn't very satisfying because she rarely obeyed me. On one occasion when we were both at school, mum had warned me that she would be late home from doing someone's hair (she was a mobile hairdresser) and so asked if I could ensure Michelle did her homework before she watched TV after school. On arriving home from school I dutifully asked her to do her homework first to which her response was to turn the TV on. I turned it off and repeated the request. She turned it back on and sat down to watch it. I turned it off and warned her that Mum would be cross. She turned it back on and completely blanked me. This continued for some time until I was seething at her wilful disobedience to my request and Mum's clear instructions and I looked forwards to mum's arrival home.

Eventually there was the sound of a key in the door and Mum walked in to find Michelle ensconced in front of the TV at which point she asked Michelle if she had done her homework. Michelle replied no she hadn't. Mum then turned the TV off and walked into the kitchen whilst instructing her to do her homework. Within seconds the sound of the TV was heard again. Mum walked back into the lounge incredulous at Michelle's barefaced disobedience and turned the TV off while telling her in no uncertain terms she was to do her homework. Michelle looked mum in the eye and said, "No! " Up until this point I had been gloating that Michelle would get her comeuppance but now I was fearful for her as she had overstepped the mark and I could see that Mum was fuming! Mum's voice was frighteningly calm as she asked her again to go and do her homework and Michelle simply lifted her chin in total defiance and refused. The next moment it was all action as Mum launched herself at Michelle to give her a smack and in the same instant Michelle saw it coming and leapt off the sofa to make her getaway.

I need to explain at this point that the ground floor of our house was like a circuit. You could pass down the hallway, into the kitchen, into the dining room then through the lounge and back into the hall. This was the route that Michelle took with mum in hot pursuit. They did a couple of laps and I stood dumbly for a couple of seconds before suddenly yelling for my sister to run faster because Mum was gaining on her. All anger at her refusal to obey me earlier had gone as I anticipated the smack she was going to get if mum ever caught up with her and this spurred me on so that I was soon jumping up and down on the spot and urging her onwards. However, she made the fatal mistake of throwing herself on the sofa and madly cycling her legs in an attempt to keep mum at bay. By this time mum was well and truly fired up and so somehow managed to avoid the tangle of flying legs enough to get a clear strike at the top of Michelle's thigh with the flat of her hand. It was a resounding slap which I imagine made Mum's hand sting as much as Michelle's leg and yet my sister only laughed in her face although I did detect a glimmer of tears in her eyes which belied the defiant laughter. Mum then told her again to go to her room and that she would not be watching any TV that night to which my sister glared at mum before storming off upstairs having conceded defeat - for now!

I want to make it clear at this point that we were not smacked often and in fact I have no recollection of being smacked although I know I was on occasions because mum has told me. This particular event is imprinted on my mind because of the sheer battle of wills that took place. I was far more compliant as a child and would never have had the strength of character to stand up to my parents as my sister did. I actually admired her spirit and her fearlessness although she did push the boundaries and I felt sorry for my parents too as they must have wondered how they managed to give birth to such a headstrong child! I think healthy discipline is a tool that all parents should use and a smack now and again certainly didn't do us any harm. In fact, Michelle would be the first to admit that she needed it. It didn't quench her fiery spirit but it held it in check at times.

I made the transition into teenage years without too much angst. I loved reading and so would happily spend hours in my room with a good book and didn't need much to entertain me. Michelle on the other hand needed firm handling and something into which she could channel her immense energy. Mum and dad thought long and hard and decided to buy Michelle a horse of her own when she was 10. Paradise Mandy was a pure bred Arab with a lovely nature albeit a bit skittish at times. She was a chestnut colour with a white blaze on her forehead and 4 white socks. Mum and dad rented a small paddock on the edge of the village and Michelle would cycle along to feed Mandy and muck out before school each morning and then repeat the process in the evenings. Mum and dad bought a small trailer and many weekends they would load Mandy up to take part in a competition somewhere in the county. Michelle loved it. She threw herself into the horsey world wholeheartedly and was soon winning rosettes for dressage and cross-country classes. My parents always asked me if I wanted to go along with them but I wasn't particularly interested in horses and so preferred my own company and that of my books. I was pleased that my sister had an interest that made her happy and that she could channel her competitive spirit into and it was great that our parents enjoyed supporting her in this new equestrian world. In hindsight I think they showed great wisdom by finding something that Michelle could focus on as otherwise her teenage years could have been potentially turbulent given her strong-willed nature.

When it came to school I was frustrated because whilst I had to work hard to attain good grades Michelle seemed to sail through everything. She too ended up being offered a place at the Girl's Grammar School in Dover and whereas I had spent my evenings as a first year closeted away with my books pouring over homework, she spent most of her time with her horse or sat in front of the TV. Mum and dad challenged her about this to which she replied she had already finished her homework. They decided to wait until the end of term exams just before Christmas fully expecting her grades to be low judging by the small amount of time she spent on her studies. This, they reasoned, would give them the ammunition they needed to force her to spend more time doing homework and less time sat in front of the TV. The weeks passed and the time for the exams came and went and then the first few results were announced. Mum and dad quizzed Michelle each day when she came home only to be told she had got brilliant grades up in the 80's and 90's so it completely stole their thunder and Michelle breezed on through her education without a worry so it seemed. I, on the other hand, invested blood, sweat and tears into my education. I can recall Michelle appearing in the doorway of my bedroom on occasions and me telling her in no uncertain terms to clear off and let me study. Just the sight of her was enough to send me into a frenzy -this little sister who could run rings around me academically and who appeared to have the world at her fingertips.

I'm not proud of myself as I recall this now but I would look for opportunities to get her into trouble with my parents. Above her bedroom door was a small glass panel so it was easy to see if the light was on in her bedroom. Michelle didn't seem to need a lot of sleep and so would stay awake long after she was meant to be asleep, reading her books, and this used to get my mum cross as she would be sluggish in the morning. Being five years my junior, her bedtime was considerably earlier than mine and so I would take great delight in creeping up the stairs and catching her with her light on when she was meant to be sleeping and then going back downstairs to report this fact to mum. Time and time again I would get her into trouble in this way which didn't lead to a happy sibling relationship. Years later she got her own back though. When I was home from college one time and in my room, Michelle appeared in the doorway and before I knew it, I was lying on my back with her sitting astride me, pinning my arms to my side. She is much stronger than me and I couldn't budge her so yelled for mum to come and get her off me. Each time I opened my mouth to shout, she would take great delight in biting off one of her fingernails and pushing it into my mouth all the while grinning and telling me it was payback time! I quickly realised my best bet was to keep my mouth tightly shut and instead hammered on the floor with my heels until mum came up to investigate all the thudding and rescued me! I have to admit it was a fair retaliation for all those times I deliberately got her into trouble by telling tales and we still laugh now about her creative way to get her own back! You don't mess with my little sister.

As I get older and the more I have glimpses into other people’s broken and messed-up lives, I have come to realise what a happy and privileged childhood we had. Home was a place of safety and security. Mum would play games with us chasing us around the house and lying in wait outside doors to make us jump and squeal with laughter. Our school friends were always welcome and I recall many a happy hour dancing to Abba records in my bedroom with my friend Julie and dreaming of one day auditioning for Pan’s People on Top of the Pops. Other times we would have to creep around the house like mice when Dad was doing a stint of night duties on the ferries and needed to sleep during the day. We enjoyed lovely family holidays in Wales and France and also in the sunny climes of the Canary Islands and Portugal on several occasions. Both sets of grandparents would come and visit regularly from

Herefordshire and we would have days out to local beaches with one of mum's famous picnics to sustain us or to some nearby beauty spot where we were let loose to roam and explore. We were set boundaries and were taught what was acceptable behaviour and what was not and we knew the consequences if we over-stepped the mark.

As adults we both have a great relationship with our parents and enjoy spending time with them. In fact, just last year when I spent a few days visiting my sister at her home near Newtown in mid Wales, we found ourselves talking about our upbringing and how grateful we are to mum and dad for their parenting skills. I was surprised to hear Michelle say that she was worried that I might have felt left out during the years that she was involved in equestrian competing while I had felt equally guilty not showing any interest! It's funny how two people can see the same set of events from totally different viewpoints. We agreed, however, that we are thankful for the work ethic mum and dad passed on to us, the ability to manage money and stay out of debt, the importance of looking after what we have and not taking it for granted, the belief in ourselves and our decisions in life, the ability to overcome fears and to achieve our dreams. We always knew we were loved. We were given space to grow. We were treated as individuals and not compared to each other. Our parents equipped us to find our own way in life but have always been there to give advice and help when needed. They allowed us to make our own choices and decisions without influencing them unduly. I hope that when they look at us, they recognise they have done a good job of parenting, and that although neither of us aspire to be parents ourselves, it's not because of anything they did wrong! When I see the baggage that many people carry today as a result of poor role models in their informative years, I am ever more grateful for the legacy of my mum and dad who instilled sound values into us and taught us not to take ourselves too seriously.

SHELLEY

Who are you I wonder, sister of mine?
I look at you and search for a sign
Of likeness in our manners or features
Yet we appear quite different creatures!
From birth you have been strong, fearless and bold –
The world failed to squeeze you into its mold;
Tenacious, you'd argue that black was white
And rarely did you concede a fight.
You travelled the world to countries far flung,
Skied snowy slopes and basked in the sun;
Climbed Kilimanjaro at dawn's first light,
Explored the Barrier Reef so bright.
The Lost City of Peru you've seen,
The Borneo jungle so lush and green;
You've ridden the Amazon's mighty swell
And the Northern Lights you've seen as well.
You seek out adventure, try all things new,
It's obvious nothing fazes you!
You dream big dreams, work hard and aspire
To change the world and set it on fire.
So little sister I want you to know
That as I have watched you blossom and grow,
You have my love and huge esteem
For all that you are and all that you mean.

Chapter Four

Jeremiah 29:11 (NLT)
For I know the plans I have for you, " says the Lord. "They are plans for good and not for disaster, to give you a future and a hope.

Driving Lessons

As a child I remember the long drive to my grandparents' house from our home in Shepherdswell in Kent to their farm on the outskirts of Hereford. They lived down a long, winding driveway off the main A49 Hereford road and I have vivid memories of my little sister at the age of seven or eight pestering dad to let her "drive ". What she meant was that she wanted to sit on his lap and steer the car down the drive while he operated the brake, clutch and accelerator as her legs were far too short to reach them. I on the other hand had no such desires and this lack of interest continued into adulthood and it was only due to the persistence of my parents that I decided to take driving lessons during my second year at college in Bath.

I had worked for a year for the hovercraft company, Hoverspeed, after leaving school and continued to get summer employment with the company during my four year degree course at Bath College of Higher Education. These savings enabled me to pay for driving lessons which my parents thought would stand me in good stead for when I acquired my first teaching post. After my initial year at Bath I moved out of the halls of residence into a 2 bedroom flat in the nearby town of Keynsham with two college friends, Anne and Jayne. I reluctantly bit the bullet and found a local driving instructor who would take me out for weekly driving lessons which I abhorred from the start. Half an hour before the scheduled start of my lesson I would feel sick and my stomach would cramp resulting in me locking myself in the bathroom. When he pulled up outside the door I would force one foot in front of the other along the hallway and out to the waiting car where he would be sat in the passenger seat and a familiar feeling of dread would wash over me. I can't actually recall his name or any interesting snippets of information about him as my focus was on getting through the hour long lesson without killing him, myself or any other innocent motorist or pedestrian. I can remember thinking that I would never master being able to steer, change gear and use the pedals all at the same time - it was just too much to think about all at once. I certainly was never a “natural “ when it came to driving and I can remember once or twice he lost his cool with me when I did something unexpected or stalled the engine several times in a row. After a considerable number of lessons (more than 20), I was put in for my first driving test in Bath and it came as no surprise to either of us that I failed. It was nearing the end of the summer term so I decided to continue with my lessons over the summer while I was at home in Shepherdswell and working back at Hoverspeed and so found another poor, unsuspecting instructor to help me achieve my goal of being able to drive.

In an attempt to encourage me in this endeavour my parents bought a second hand dark blue Vauxhall Polo which they insured for me to drive in order to supplement my lessons. I would catch the train into work in Dover in the morning and then when I arrived home in the evening my dad would suggest that we go out for a drive to give me some practice. Now, I have already mentioned that patience was not one of my dad's strong points and so as I walked home from the train station I would be frantically dreaming up some excuse as to why I couldn't go out driving. However, I rarely came up with a feasible argument and so after delaying the inevitable for as long as I could, my dad would come and find me and suggest it was time for a little drive. My heart would sink but I'd try and persuade myself that it wouldn't be too bad and the sooner we started, the sooner I would be home.

Actually getting off the driveway was a feat in itself. Our house was situated at the top of the hill in the village and on a sharp corner. I had to reverse the car as far away from the corner as possible while still staying on the driveway frontage before pulling away swiftly onto the opposite side of the road to avoid any vehicles that might come hurtling around the corner. It was made increasingly stressful by the fact that the little blue Polo had a tendency to stall (this was not just down to my poor clutch control but something which my mum struggled with too!) which in turn made me more jittery. Once safely off the driveway I would try and relax but to relax behind the wheel of a car seemed an anathema to me! We would drive along the country lanes surrounding the village where I lived and I clearly remember a particularly nasty junction on a steep incline in the nearby village of Eythorne. The road passed over a railway line and so when a train was coming the barriers were lowered and the cars would have to wait until the train passed. On one occasion I happened to be at the front of the queue as the London-bound train passed with a convoy of several cars behind me. As the barriers were lifted, I put the car into first gear and attempted to pull away smoothly uphill only to kangaroo jump forward before stalling the engine. This humiliating process was then repeated several more times as I became increasingly aware of the other drivers behind me which in turn added to my stress levels. I begged Dad to take over and told him I couldn't do it but he refused point blank to swap seats with me and told me in no uncertain terms that we would sit there all day if necessary until I mastered hill-starts! I was mortified and burst into tears but he didn't relent and eventually, after what seemed like a lifetime, I succeeded in pulling away without stalling.

According to Dad I had an unnerving tendency to accelerate when really I should be slowing down. On the narrow country lanes there was often only just room for cars to pass but when I saw a car coming towards me instead of dropping my speed and giving myself time to assess the width of the gap, I would put my foot on the accelerator and just go for it with Dad beside me braking like mad and yelling at me to slow down. I think in all honesty Dad did try not to raise his voice at me but it must have been difficult when his delinquent daughter seemed determined to kill him in a head-on collision.

Driving practice with Mum was a different thing altogether. Mum wasn't as confident as Dad at taking me out driving as she felt vulnerable without having any controls herself but she was a much calmer teacher and didn't raise her voice to me. On arriving home from work in the evening I would beg her to take me out instead of Dad as I recognised Mum's teaching methods were more suited to my nervous disposition than Dad's and I didn't tend to get as uptight. Reluctantly she would agree and we would set off with me feeling a lot calmer and her no doubt feeling anxious. I have such hilarious memories of times spent with her in the passenger seat as she would tell me to turn left or right at the next junction and when I reached it I would decide I didn't like the look of it and simply kept going! We used to go for miles out of our way simply because I would panic and avoid certain roads because I knew there was a hill start or a roundabout to negotiate. Dad would never have entertained it and I would have been too scared not to do as he instructed but Mum was a different kettle of fish! I also remember on one occasion when we came to a junction which was on a nasty corner, mum got out and stood on the far side of the road to see me out safely. As I swung out wide to turn I nearly ran her over and she had to leap back onto the verge to avoid getting mown down! Thankfully I remembered to stop so that she could get back in although she probably would have preferred not to! Another time the sun was very low in the sky and as I hurtled down a country lane mum commented she couldn't see anything because the sun was blinding her. My reply was that I couldn't see anything either which for some reason didn't seem to instil confidence into her! We would often end up in helpless tears of laughter at the end of a driving session with Mum a bag of nerves and me feeling relaxed and actually beginning to think that this driving thing wasn't so bad after all.

Before heading back to college at the end of the summer break I was put in for my test again. This time I took it in Canterbury which is where I had been having lessons supplemented by practice sessions with mum and dad. At the end of the test when I had answered a few questions, the examiner passed me and I breathed a sigh of relief as I stepped out of the car and went to tell my instructor the good news. When I got home I told mum who found it hard to believe despite me showing her the evidence and I think Dad was equally surprised - I imagine they had all but given up hope of me ever being in possession of a driving licence. They weren't the only ones!

I am so glad now that I faced my fears and actually leant to drive as we live on a farm that is 2 miles from the nearest public bus-stop and 4 miles from the nearest town. I can't even begin to imagine what it would be like if I didn't have the independence of being able to get in a car and drive. There is a lesson in that. There will always be things in life that stretch us and take us out of our comfort zones but God does it for a reason. He knew that when I was in my early 20's I needed a driving license because he could see my future. He knew I would meet and marry Tim, that I would be living in a remote farmhouse where a car was a necessity rather than a luxury and he helped me to confront and overcome my fear. The following poem talks about the various fears in life that can assail us at different seasons but the antidote is the same in each case – trust God and allow him to walk each dark valley with you. He won't take the fear away, but he will be by your side each step of the way, holding your hand and calming your anxious heart.

FEAR
Its disguises are many, its effect is the same -
This immobilising force which has 'fear' as its name.
Fear of being ridiculed for the things you believe,
Fear of bereavement and of being left to grieve.
Fear of persecution for daring to speak your mind,
Fear of growing older and of running out of time.
Fear of unemployment or enforced redundancy,
Fear of failing health or a disabling injury.

Fear of rejection, of being unloved and alone,
Fear of repossession and of losing your home.
Our daily lives are brimming with worries and concerns
Crowding in around us so we don't know where to turn,
But there's someone who can help you overcome your fears,
He's waiting to console you and wipe away your tears.
His name is Jesus, God's beloved Son and heir -
He's reaching out to touch your life and show that He cares.
So what will you do? Will you offer Him your life
And ask Him to help you overcome your fears and strife?
Or will you turn your back and choose to go your own way
With life's fears overwhelming you as you face each day?
So think about the options, only you can decide -
Will you open up the door or leave Him stood outside?

For those of you who are reading this book without ever having been a passenger in my car, don't let my stories deter you from either learning to drive yourself or from allowing me to be your chauffeur! I have been driving for many years now and despite my misgivings of ever being able to co-ordinate the gears, steering and foot pedals, I can assure you it did finally all "click " and I actually quite enjoy driving now both on the quiet country lanes and the faster motorways. In fact, just this past week Tim and I were able to spend a week on Anglesey with my parents and sister and I took them out in the car for the day with my dad sat in the passenger seat reminiscing about bygone days in the blue Vauxhall Polo. He tried telling me my driving hadn't improved much until I threatened to make him walk home at which point he conceded I wasn't a bad driver - true praise indeed!

Chapter Five

Ecclesiastes 2:3 (NLT)
After much thought, I decided to cheer myself with wine. And while still seeking wisdom, I clutched at foolishness. In this way, I tried to experience the only happiness most people find during their brief life in this world.

The College Years

I can still remember the sinking feeling in my stomach as I watched my parents drive away and leave me.

I had arrived at Bath College of Higher Education on the outskirts of that beautiful city near the picturesque village of Newton-St-Loe. After signing in at reception, I was allocated a room, N7 in Langton Court, into which I emptied the contents of my parents' car boot. Next door to my room was the toilet which served the 5 rooms on the first floor and along the corridor was the tiny kitchen for the whole block of 10 rooms. The bathroom was at the far end of the corridor and each room had its own sink. The furniture in each room consisted of a bed, a desk, a sink built into a wardrobe unit and a shelf along one wall. It was basic but clean and would be my home for the next 12 months. Once I had found homes for my clothes, food, books and toiletries, my parents and I walked around the site to enable me to acclimatise myself and then before I knew it I was waving them off down the long driveway for the 3 hour drive back to Kent. Feeling a little overwhelmed by the finality of it all, I returned to my room to do some more sorting and to make myself a cup of tea and it wasn't long before there was a tap at the door and I opened it to find a short, dark-haired girl stood on the landing. She introduced herself as Rachel and informed me she was also a first year and her room was across the courtyard on the ground floor. She had been studying the room plan we had been given on arrival and realised that we were two of only three B.Ed. first years in Langton Court so had come to seek me out. I invited her in and offered her a cup of tea and with that simple gesture our friendship was cemented. We then went together to meet the other first year student who was upstairs in Rachel's block and whose name was Rosie. By the time I went to bed that night I had two new friends and my first night at college didn't seem quite so lonely.

The next day all the first years made their way to the main hall where we were to register for our various courses and be given our timetables. As I was standing in the queue, I got talking to another girl in front of me whose name was Anne and who, it turned out, was also doing the B.Ed. course in primary school teaching. We hit it off straight away and after registration she invited me back to see her room in Sidney Court which my bedroom window overlooked. We were to become firm friends and later, after moving out of halls of residence, we would share a house together for three years.

Fresher’s Week seemed to pass in a blur as various activities were organised and then we soon settled into the routine of lectures and got to know our way around the campus. There was a small farm connected with the college and during my first week I found myself heading in that direction. I wandered around until a jovial faced man with an unruly mop of curls and dressed in overalls and Wellington boots approached and asked me if he could help me. His name was John Peters and he was the Farm Manager. I explained that my grandfather had managed a small farm and that I loved animals and wondered if there was anything I could help with before lectures each day. He seemed quite bemused by my offer of free labour and said I was welcome to help collect eggs and clean out the chicken shed. The next day before lectures began I turned up for duty and was shown the ropes by a young employee called Adrian who worked full time on the farm. This then became my regular routine. I would get up early and walk down to the farm to work before starting lectures at 9am or 10am. The farm manager, John, was lovely as was his wife, Joan, who worked in the college canteen. I became friends with his younger daughter, Sharon, who was a year younger than me. Sharon had special educational needs due to problems when she was born but loved the farm and liked nothing better than to drive tractors in the fields under Adrian's close supervision. She was a larger-than-life personality who was very loud and had a very severe, penetrating stare which many people who didn't know her found unnerving. Once she got to know me and trust me she would often walk down to my room in the hall of residence, talking to herself all the while or singing loudly and tunelessly so that I often heard her before I saw her. It wasn't until many months into the course that I discovered that some of the other students thought I was someone important and that Sharon was my bodyguard! When I explained the misunderstanding to her we both had a good laugh.

On one occasion when I went home to Kent I asked John if I could take Sharon with me for the weekend. He agreed and so we set off from Bath to London on the train. Once we arrived at Paddington Station we both went to use the facilities before the next leg of the journey down to Shepherdswell and I impressed upon Sharon the importance of waiting for me but to my horror when I came out of my toilet cubicle she was nowhere to be seen! I waited for some time not sure what to do next and imagining how I would explain to John that I had lost his daughter in the middle of London bearing in mind she hadn't been much further than Bath before! As I stood thinking through my options (this was pre-mobile phones) I became aware of a commotion up on the platform and recognised Sharon's voice admonishing herself for not doing as I had asked. I had never been so pleased to hear her and was too relieved to tell her off and thankfully the rest of the journey passed uneventfully.

Sharon liked to smoke and would make her own roll-ups with great dexterity but I had warned her that she wouldn't be able to smoke in my parents' house and would have to go outside in the garden. She accepted this without argument but my mum felt mean making her go out in the cold to have a cigarette and so relented and let her smoke in the utility room. Sharon would remind me of this often when we got back to college telling everyone that I was a "tight bugger " because I had told her to smoke outside but that my mum was nice and had let her stay inside! That was the one and only time Sharon came home with me but she has never forgotten it and still talks about me losing her at Paddington Station. Another memory that sticks in my mind is when she was bridesmaid for her sister, Nicola. The wedding took place in June in the tiny parish church of Newton-St-Loe and it was the only time I have ever seen Sharon in a dress. She was to accompany the best man down the aisle after the bride and groom but was quite overcome by the emotion of the occasion. Her face puckered and she howled loudly the whole length of the church, drowning out the music and leaving the poor best man at a loss of how to console her and quieten her down. It was a wedding march I won't forget in a hurry!

After leaving college and getting my first teaching post, I have kept in touch with Sharon over the years. Now, more than twenty years later, she lives in a residential home in Swansea and comes to visit me several times a year with her care worker and we often reminisce about those college days in Bath.

In the early days I attended the local church service and even took Sharon with me on one or two occasions. She wasn't impressed and it was difficult to keep her from disappearing outside for a smoke so I didn't pursue that one. But now I had a new life of freedom and since none of my new friends had any interest in going to church, it didn't take long for me to forget about God and leave him on the side-lines of my life. A couple of months after starting college I was going out with Adrian, the lad who worked on the farm, and evenings would be spent drinking together in the Student Union Bar or down at the local Social Club which we had access to due to Sharon and her dad being members there. I fell head over heels in love and in my naivety thought we were going to live the happy ever after life. We talked about the future, about getting married and having our own farm one day and it wasn't long before he was staying overnight despite it being against college rules. At the time I thought I was being mature and grown up, making my own decisions, forging my own pathway through life. I knew it wasn't God's desire for me but I managed to drown out the voice of my conscience and told myself it would be fine because we would get married one day after I had graduated. However, several months into our relationship I suspected Adrian of being unfaithful with one of my friends and so I called it off. He denied anything happened between them but they had both been drinking and he spent most of the night in her room so I didn't give him the benefit of the doubt. I was heartbroken. All my dreams lay in pieces at my feet and I felt used and battered. I found myself crying all the time, I didn't want to spend time with my friends, I lost all interest in food and consequently lost a lot of weight and felt that my world had ended. It was during this time that I wrote the following poem in which captures a little bit of the pain and confusion I was feeling;

LOST LOVE
Anguish stabs deeper into my soul,
Pain sears through my grieving body,
Is this what love is all about?
Hot tears forge salty rivulets
But the storm within me does not abate.
How can emotions be so fickle?
Yesterday the future was bright and rosy,
Love coloured everything with a pink tinge.
Today I'm left feeling empty and gutted
As the sun disappears and the sky turns black.
Somewhere within me a voice is crying -
A banshee wail of torment and despair,
No words of solace can ease my grief;
I exist alone in the inky blackness,
An empty shell floating on a restless sea.

As the months passed and time began its healing process, you would have thought that this experience would have been enough to throw me back on God but unfortunately it didn't. I think I must have been a slow learner because it took me more than four years to realise that I was clutching at foolishness (Ecclesiastes 2:3) and that a life without God in it was empty and meaningless. Instead I threw myself into the student culture of excess alcohol and multiple relationships. Once we moved out of the halls of residence at the end of the first year, three of us friends got a ground floor flat together in the nearby town of Keynsham. Anne and I shared a room and the other girl, Jayne, had her own room as she was a smoker. The partying continued with us often catching the bus into Bath on a Saturday night to frequent the various night clubs there and then sharing a taxi home or simply crashing on the floor of some friends' house. During the week we would go to the local pubs where it was not unusual for me to be drunk to the extent that I remember on one occasion being egged on to arm wrestle with another girl on the floor of the pub! I think somewhere at the back of my mind I knew this was not the life that God had planned for me but I managed to successfully tune out the voice that was trying to make itself heard above the call of worldly pleasure. I continued to clutch at foolishness and to cheer myself with wine and relationships and if anyone had at that point in my life foretold that one day I would end up being a pastor's wife, I would have laughed in their face. My life style was certainly not conducive to that of a spiritual leader in any shape, way or form - I was living for me and for the moment and convincing myself that I was happy and fulfilled. Somehow I managed to juggle this lifestyle of excess with managing to get assignments handed in on time (just) and completing my blocks of teaching practice which were totally exhausting. After four years I graduated with a 2nd class B.Ed. (honours) degree and was about as far away from God as I could be.

Some years ago I saw a powerful performance on you tube which conveys this struggle. It is a mime put to the song “Everything “ by Lighthouse. God is in the background trying to make himself known as various figures which represent sex, money, alcohol and despair try to keep the young woman from him. It depicted very clearly what my life looked like at this point in the journey and made me cry as I realised how hard God had been battling on my behalf and yet I failed to see the loving arms that were longing to wrap themselves around me and protect me from my poor choices and subsequent pain. The amazing thing is that God is a God of second chances. He is more interested in our future than our past. When we come to him and admit our mistakes and ask for his forgiveness the Bible says he remembers them no more (Hebrews 8:12) or as Psalm 103:12 says, " He has removed our sins as far from us as the east is from the west. "

Yes, we are in a battle but victory is ours if we swap our dirty rags for the pure white robes of righteousness that Jesus longs to give us.

BATTLEGROUND
Each direction I turn, enemies surround,
I feel I'm alone in this dark battleground.
Busyness attacks first, selling me the lie
That I can pray later when I've got more time.
The telephone rings, there's someone at the door,
Pressure is mounting, I can't cope anymore!
Guilt then appears to add his weight to the fray
Asking, "Did you have a quiet time today? "
The answer is, "No! " so a failure I feel –
Once again I've let God down, is my faith real?
Doubt assails me then, such a powerful foe,
Telling me I'm useless, making me feel low,
Questioning my worthiness, "Why would God love me? "
I've been badly wounded, is it fatally?
Joy and peace are gone, the battle's nearly lost
But as I lift me eyes I see a wooden cross.
The figure hanging there turns to meet my gaze
And God's love reaches out through the darkening haze;
Piercing my heart with such overwhelming grace
That Guilt and Fear are forced to cover their face.
My strength flows back, the cross gives me new power –
In God will I trust, my refuge and strong tower.

Chapter Six

Romans 8:1 (NLT)
So now there is no condemnation for those who belong to Christ Jesus.

A New Start

Following my Graduation I started applying for teaching jobs and was invited for interview at Picklenash Junior School in Newent, Gloucestershire. I didn't get the job that had been advertised but I did get a 12 month post that they were also wanting to fill and so at the end of August I found myself moving into a tiny annexe built onto the side of my new landlady's house. Fortunately for me one of the other teachers happened to live right next door so I soon had a lift into school each morning. I know I didn't feel very prepared on that first morning as I waited for the bell to ring signalling the start of the new term and my first meeting with the children in my class. I had been given a Year 3 class who were just starting at the junior school so we were all going to have to learn the ropes together. As a probationary teacher I had also been allocated a mentor, a diminutive woman called Ann Shaw, who taught the other Year 3 class next door to mine. She was to be an excellent role model and a wonderful source of advice and she helped me tremendously during my first year of teaching. I had a class of 23 children that first year and I can still remember most of their names nearly 25 years later! I still bump into one or two of them from time to time and can remember one occasion a burly young man stood at the bank cashier next to me asking tentatively, "I don't suppose you remember me do you Miss? " As it turned out I knew exactly who he was and was able to respond with his name which he seemed very pleased about. I loved teaching and threw myself into it whole-heartedly.

Living on my own in my little annexe meant that I had plenty of time to think. I didn't know anyone else in Newent apart from the staff at the school and so my evenings would be spent marking books and preparing lessons for the next day. At the time I was going out with Jon, who I had met in a local village pub during my third year at college and he would come up to visit me at weekends from time to time but other than that my social life was pretty non-existent. My thoughts went back to my life pre-college and I thought I would try and reconnect with a church family because I felt something was missing from my life. I attended the local Anglican Church in the town for a few weeks and was made to feel very welcome by the elderly congregation but although I was familiar with the service, there was no-one there my age. About this time, the special needs teacher at the school, Andrea Hayden, came alongside me one day and invited me for tea at her house. She was a widow whose minister husband had died of cancer when their only daughter, Ruth, was four years old and she had moved to Newent to find work. Andrea was one of the liveliest and most energetic people I had ever met and we soon became good friends as she took me under her wing. She was a committed Christian and it wasn't long before she invited me to go with her to her church one Sunday evening which I was happy to do. It was an independent evangelical church and immediately I was struck by how many young people there were there compared to what I had experienced at the Anglican Church. After the service a couple of the young people approached me and invited me back to someone's house for something called "Afterchurch " which was a social time for the younger members of the church. I agreed to go and was immediately made to feel one of the gang as we chatted, played games and had something to eat. Two of the girls, Paula and Ashley, also lived on their own and so the three of us became good friends and would meet up during the week as well as at church on Sundays.

As I started listening to the messages each week my understanding of the Bible grew and I felt convicted about my relationship with Jon. He had proposed on two occasions and I had refused because I didn't feel sure he was the right one for me. I tried to analyse my emotions and realised that he was the only familiar thing in my life which was why I struggled to let go of the relationship. I had recently started a new job and career, moved to a completely new area, found a new church and started making new friends and he was my only tie to the past. However, I realised that I didn't see a future together for us and so it was time to cut the ties. When Jon next came to visit me we had a long, candid chat and although it was painful for both of us I think we both knew it was the right decision. I felt as if God was saying to me, “So far but no further my girl! “ I had lived the past four years on my terms thinking they would bring happiness but instead I had made countless stupid decisions and choices, I had hurt people and been hurt myself. God had watched all this from the side-lines of my life, silently sorrowing over my selfish, destructive behaviour until he could bear it no longer. He orchestrated my job in Newent where he planned for me to meet Andrea who would then introduce me to Glebe Chapel which was to be my spiritual home for the next decade. I don't believe in co-incidence but I do believe in God-incidence and I thank God that he brought healing to my life and freed me from that downward spiral.

If I'm honest I feel I totally wasted my years at college. When I hear of young Christians who go away to university and head up Christian Unions or lead ministries in churches I feel ashamed of my behaviour. I could have been salt and light amongst my peers and could have shared God's love with them but instead I allowed the world to push me into its mold and I certainly didn't bring glory to his name - quite the opposite. However, I know I can't change the past but I can resolve to do better in the future with God's grace. He has redeemed me, he has called me by name and I am his. He has a plan and purpose for my life and I need to keep moving forwards into that plan rather than wasting time and energy regretting the past about which I can do nothing. If I feel moments of condemnation I have come to realise they are from Satan and so have no part in my life - I choose to claim the grace and freedom found in Christ instead. I once wrote a poem which seeks to explain these feelings and have included it here.

HAUNTED
Fragmented memories of the past
Flash across my consciousness
Like glass splinters;
Vivid images of carnal desires,
Echoes of conversations
Coloured with lies and deceit.
Shameful memories, best forgotten
Locked in the dark recesses of my soul
Unleashed like vengeful spirits
To haunt my peace of mind.
Sullied and tarnished, I stand accused,
Knowing the verdict is 'Guilty'.
Yet I dare to hold my head up high,
For the slate is washed clean
By the precious blood of my Redeemer
Gone are the ghosts -
Banished by sacrificial love.

One May evening after having had a meal at Andrea's house, there was a knock at her door and a young man entered for the Sunday School teachers' meeting that she was hosting. We passed in the narrow hallway, me on the way out and Tim on the way in. It transpired sometime later that his first impression of me was "teeth and hair " which wasn't the most romantic or flattering compliment! I remember noticing him after this in church on Sundays but we didn't interact much and quietly watched each other from a distance. So the months continued. I joined in with the various activities that the young people at church planned, I attended church on Sunday mornings and Sunday evenings and I thrived on the Bible teaching that was refreshing, relevant and practical. Tim was often part of the group of young people but I was still recovering from my break up with Jon and Tim had ended a relationship with a long-term girlfriend and so neither of us were looking to get involved with anyone just yet. However, God had different plans.

I regularly used to get invitations back to peoples' homes for lunch on Sundays as they knew I was on my own and on one such Sunday Tim's sister-in-law, Helen, invited me to their house. When I got there I was surprised to find that Tim had been invited too. We had a lovely lunch and then Tim announced that he was on milking duty (he and his two brothers were partners in a dairy farm) and asked did I want to help him? With my love of animals and background in farming I jumped at the chance and so we spent the afternoon in the milking parlour with 150 cows - not really the most romantic or aromatic of surroundings! I soon got the hang of putting machines on and dipping the cows' teats in iodine once they had finished milking before they were let out back into the fields. I don't have any recollections of any other interactions at that time but the next event in our developing friendship occurred in February.

It was Valentine's Day and I was the happy recipient of 3 Valentine's cards! One was placed under my car window wipers when it was parked in the local Christian bookshop car park, one was delivered by the postman and the other was pushed under the door of my annexe. I worked out who the first two were from but was completely flummoxed by the third one. I pondered on it for a week or more but was no closer to an answer and it was really frustrating me. One evening nearly two weeks later I was given another clue in the form of another note pushed under the door. It was a piece of paper with the logo of "Send a Cow " charity on it which I knew was a Christian charity that Tim's father was one of the directors of and the message scribbled on it read, "This is one almighty clue! " Well, I didn't think Tim's dad was likely to be sending me a Valentine's card so the obvious conclusion was that it was Tim! I must confess I was more than a little surprised as he had kept his distance but I was quite impressed with his creativity and the effort he had put into maintaining the mystery.

It wasn't long after this that we started going out together although neither of us have any recollections of any particular dates. I was busy most evenings doing schoolwork and Tim was busy on the farm so we tended to grab a couple of hours in an evening whenever we could. I do remember very clearly though after our first evening spent together that Tim suggested we pray together before he went home. I was completely taken aback. I had had lots of boyfriends, none of them Christians, and so had never heard of praying together - it was a completely novel concept but I could tell he was serious. That set a precedent for the rest of our lives together. It took me a while to feel comfortable and confident to pray out loud in front of Tim but it is a habit we have adopted from that moment and one which I would encourage all couples to work on. It may feel awkward and embarrassing to begin with but it soon becomes easier and is the cement that holds marriages together. We usually pray together when we go to bed and our usual practice is for Tim to pray first and then me. On more than one occasion I have fallen asleep during Tim's prayer and when there is no response from me when he says "Amen ", he says it again a little louder which then usually elicits a sleepy "Amen " from me! Even worse is when I fall asleep in the middle of my own prayer!

In those early days we would spend hours sat in the car talking about Christian issues, sharing our past experiences and discussing dreams and plans for the future. Tim had grown up in a strong Christian family, his parents, siblings and most of his extended family were all evangelical Christians who spoke about their faith openly. I had grown up with grandparents and my mum who had a quiet personal faith but who didn't talk about it much and my own faith journey had been very up and down. We were two very different people with two very different backgrounds and yet God had brought us together and so when Tim proposed just 2 months after we started dating, I had no hesitation in saying, "Yes! " My parents were still living in Kent at the time and so we planned to tell them of our plans over the summer when we met up. However, the next occasion that we visited Kent was for my sister's 21st birthday celebrations in July and we didn't feel it was right to announce our news then and steal the limelight. The next opportunity didn't arise until my parents came to visit my grandparents in the September. I invited them over to my tiny annexe for a meal and the plan was that Tim would ask my dad for my hand in marriage - simple we thought! The evening arrived and my parents arrived at the time we had arranged but there was no sign of Tim. I know things can sometimes crop up at the last minute in farm life so I wasn't too perturbed, made a pot of tea and sat chatting with mum and dad. Half an hour passed, an hour, still no Tim. At this point I was feeling a little concerned but suggested we go ahead and eat dinner otherwise it would spoil. We ate dinner followed by dessert and still there was no sign of him. I didn't feel it was right for me to tell them of our plans and at this point it did cross my mind that maybe he had got cold feet and had changed his mind. I mentally replayed the conversation with him early in our relationship in which I had admitted I hadn’t kept myself pure for marriage and began to wonder if he had belatedly baulked at my revelation. I apologised to my parents that the evening hadn't gone as planned and they put their coats on to leave as they had to drive back to my grandparents’ house near Hereford. Just as they were going out of the door a rather flustered looking Tim appeared around the corner explaining that he had broken down on the tractor in a field several miles from the farm and had had to walk back home. This was pre-mobile phones so he had no way of letting me know what had happened! He asked my parents to stay a few minutes longer as there was something he wanted to talk to them about. They obligingly came back in and he asked my dad if he could marry me much to mum's surprise as she really had no idea that we had an ulterior motive for the evening. She was sent into even more of a tail spin when we announced our intention to get married in April - just over six months away! The evening's events should have set red warning lights flashing in my mind as during our 22 years of married life the biggest cause of stress on my part is Tim being late for things! But as the saying goes, “Love is blind! “

Chapter Seven

Psalm 127:1a (NLT)
Unless the Lord builds a house,
the work of the builders is wasted.

A Farmer's Wife

Tim and I were married on Easter Saturday, 10th April 1993 in the parish church of Much Dewchurch - the church which I had attended with my grandad and where as a child I had been christened. It was a beautiful day which passed in a bit of a blur. I had two bridesmaids, my sister and my college friend Anne and our page boy was Tim's two-year-old nephew Nathan. Tim recalls feeling really nervous the evening before the wedding so gave his car a good wash to calm him. Surprisingly I can't remember feeling nervous at all after my reservations about previous boyfriends - I just knew that we were meant to be together. The reception took place at Symonds Yat West on the picturesque River Wye and in the evening we had a barn dance led by Tim's old primary School headmaster, Dick Brice who is a bit of a legend in the Forest of Dean. I don't remember much about the speeches other than dad asking for some cows for my dowry which he claims he is still waiting for and taking inflation into account he thinks he should have a couple more now! It was a wonderful, happy occasion and at the end of the evening we took our leave and stayed one night in a local hotel near Ross before leaving for a week in the Lake District the following day.

On that first night we were given a complimentary bottle of

champagne in a bucket of ice to celebrate our wedding day but we decided to take it with us the following day instead. When we arrived at our B&B in Borrowdale that evening we thought we'd celebrate with the champagne but hadn't taken into account it was no longer chilled! As Tim removed the wire, the cork flew out of its own volition, ricocheted off the ceiling (narrowly missing the light) and a plume of frothy champagne drenched the bed! We didn't quite know how we were going to explain our champagne soaked bed to the proprietors but they were very understanding and happily changed the sheets for us. The room still smelt a bit like a brewery the next morning though!

Between our engagement and wedding day I had moved out of the annexe and into a furnished first floor flat in Gorsley, only a mile or so from the farm. After the tiny dimensions of the annexe this seemed like a mansion and to begin with I would just wander from room to room enjoying the space. Once we were married Tim moved in as the plan was to do some renovations to the farmhouse where he had been living with his parents and to make it into two houses, one for us and one for them. This process took the best part of 18 months but we were very happy in our flat as we adjusted to married life. I continued to teach at Highnam Primary School where I had secured a job after my probationary year in Newent and the children made the transition from calling me Miss Price to Mrs Cracknell. Tim continued to work on the farm with his two brothers and adjusted well to the mile-long commute instead of merely stepping out of the front door each day into the farmyard!

It was during this period that I made the decision to be baptised. I had been christened as a baby and then confirmed when I was thirteen in the Parish church in Shepherdswell and so didn't see the need for baptism as well. However, after attending a baptism service at Glebe Chapel in Newent, I started feeling an unrest and so began a silent battle with God. Since my introduction to Glebe Chapel my spiritual growth had taken on a vibrancy as I discovered new truths about God and developed the habit of a daily time spent with him, reading my Bible and praying. I was enjoying this new stage of the journey but at the same time it was challenging and made me examine myself and address issues of pride and stubbornness. Finally, while reading my Bible early one morning, I was convicted that it was a step of obedience I needed to take and so I bounced into the bedroom where Tim was still sleeping, clambered on the bed and announced to my sleepy husband that I was going to be baptised. After his rude awakening and initial surprise, Tim admitted that he had been praying that it was a decision I would come to although he hadn't once mentioned it to me. He knew even in those early days of marriage that I didn't like to be told what to do and that if he pushed me in that direction I was likely to dig my heels in and refuse to oblige. And so it was that on 2nd January 1994 I was baptised at Glebe Chapel in Newent by my father-in-law and my brother-in-law, Ian, and I was given the baptism verse of Galatians 2:20 which says; "My old self has been crucified with Christ. It is no longer I who live, but Christ lives in me. So I live in this earthly body by trusting in the Son of God, who loved me and gave himself for me. "

Once the renovations had been done we moved in to our new home at the farm. The original farmhouse was called Withymoor Farm and we had to think of a name for our half of the house and decided upon Withyland Heights as I had romantic ideas about Charlotte Bronte's novel 'Wuthering Heights'. The move was an easy one. We inherited the furniture that Tim's parents left behind so at least the rooms were partially furnished and we added to it from charity shops and from what was passed on to us from friends and family. I loved the big, airy rooms of the farmhouse and living in the midst of farm life with its noise and its smells. Apparently my mum reminded me that when I was thirteen I had announced to her that when I was older I was going to marry a Welsh sheep farmer so I wasn't too far out when I married a Herefordian dairy farmer!

Those first few years on the farm found me trying my hand at decorating for the first time. Each school holiday I would tackle another room in the house, ripping off aged wall paper (often up to five layers of it!), polyfilling cracks and holes and choosing light pastel shades to paint the walls with. Being an old house it was never straight forward as I uncovered wattle and daub plaster with tufts of horse hair sticking out of it which then had to be completely removed and replastered. One amazing discovery we made was the huge inglenook fireplace in what had been Tim's dad's office and which became our lounge. It had been hidden by a much smaller fireplace which once removed revealed a beautiful Gorsley stone fireplace with original oak beam lintel. Needless to say we told the builder to leave it uncovered and later we paid £50 for a huge, cast iron log burner to be installed which would emit enough heat to melt the candles on the other side of the room! Every task was nearly always a much bigger job than I had anticipated and I was appreciative of my parents' help at various stages in this on-going renovation project. However, after spending our combined savings on completely re-wiring the house and installing double glazing and additional central heating, it felt like I was making my mark on our home.

For part of our wedding present my sister-in-law, Helen, had made a cross-stitch for us depicting the words from Psalm 127 which talks about the importance of God building the house and this was a timely reminder that no matter what wonderful transformations I managed to achieve, our house needed to have God at its centre. During these early stages of married life we often opened up our home on a Sunday evening to the young people's "Afterchurch " gatherings which had first made me feel so welcome when I was a young, single teacher looking for friends. I felt a sense that God had given us a lovely home and I wanted to share it with others so we would often have people around for meals and that is something I have enjoyed doing all through our married life. When Tim and I first got married my intention was to fatten him up and so I would practice making home-baked cakes and cookies which he obligingly tucked into without too many complaints. Now nearly 23 years down the line he says that I have done too good a job and he is trying to cut down on his calorie intake in order to reduce his growing waistline. As I love baking and find it very therapeutic it now means that others are on the receiving end of my rock cakes, coconut cookies, chocolate brownies and Victoria sponges and I've been told I have a ministry of baking as I turn up at someone's front door bearing a tin containing home-baked goodies. If there is no response to my knock, I leave the tin on the doorstep and it is duly returned to me empty several days later.

Initially, I wanted everything to be just right when we had visitors; the house had to be tidy with no muddles, the food delicious and beautifully served up so I put a lot of pressure on myself because I wanted people to think I was a good wife. However, as the years have passed I have come to realise that God is more interested in relationships and it's not how tidy my house is or how delicious the meal, but more to do with am I relaxed enough to really listen to our guests and give them my undivided attention? Do they feel at ease or are they too scared to kick their shoes off or move a cushion in case they make a muddle? I still have a picture in my mind of one occasion when I was expecting friends for lunch and had carefully vacuumed the lounge carpet so that it had lovely even stripes in the thick pile and looked like a newly mown lawn. I went to check on something in the kitchen and came back to find Tim walking over my vacuumed floor deliberately rubbing out the lines with his feet! I wasn't impressed and asked him what on earth he was doing to which he replied it looked too neat and tidy and people wouldn't feel at home! Whilst on the one hand I was hopping mad, on reflection (and I've never admitted this to him!) I could see his point.

I am always chastised when I read the account of Jesus' visit to his friend Lazarus's house when the two sisters, Martha and Mary have such different responses to his arrival. Martha is sent into a tail spin as she rushes around trying to scrape together a meal to feed the hungry crowd while Mary sits at Jesus' feet and drinks in his words. Naturally I am a Martha, a doer, a task-oriented personality whose love language is acts of service. However, I hear Jesus' words in Luke 10 loud and clear, "But the Lord said to her, "My dear Martha, you are worried and upset over all these details! There is only one thing worth being concerned about. Mary has discovered it, and it will not be taken away from her. " When I find myself stressing over some aspect of hospitality, I remind myself that I need to get my focus back on Jesus and off the perceived problem. I want my home to be a sanctuary, a safe place, a retreat, a place where God is and where healing can take place. I want it to be filled with the aroma of Christ not furniture polish and air freshener. I hear the gentle rebuke and the sadness in Jesus words and ask him to help me be still, to stop stressing and to simply enjoy his presence as I spend time with Christian friends.

As new neighbours, I must state also that my parents-in-law couldn't have been more supportive. They told me from the moment we moved in to our half of the farmhouse that I was free to do what I wanted. They didn't want me to think I had to smuggle pieces of unwanted furniture out of the house in the dark of night for fear of upsetting them - the furniture they left was simply to tide us over until we could afford to buy our own. In fact, they took an active interest in the changes I was making to their old home and would often come and inspect the handiwork of their new daughter-in-law. I can remember coming home from school on more than one occasion after we discovered the inglenook fireplace to find Tim's dad stood in the doorway looking in wonder at our transformed lounge and he would often jokingly tell visitors to the house that I had “ruined “ a perfectly good office. I have been asked on several occasions if I find it hard living so close to my in-laws and I can honestly say I never have and in my experience it has many benefits. When I was teaching full time I would hang out a load of washing on the line before leaving for school and would come home to find it aired and folded neatly in a basket inside my front door. When I ran the Bed & Breakfast business and we had guests arriving while we were out, I could always rely on Tim's mum to show them in and make them feel at home. Until recently, Tim's dad has seen it as his job to mow the shared back lawn which, if you know our garden, is no mean feat! It takes more than 2 hours to do on a good day and considerably longer if it hasn't been done for a while! No, in all honesty I feel blessed to have such loving, thoughtful and caring parents-in-law and it is a privilege, not a hardship, to live next door to them.

Tim often jokes that once I had “caught “ him, I lost all interest in farming and rarely got involved with milking the cows but that isn't strictly true. In those early days of marriage I would quite often help at weekends with feeding the calves and bedding them down. I even wrote a poem describing these weekend duties and have included it here;

MY FAVOURITE HAT
It's hanging there in the hallway
On the peg behind the front door,
My multi-coloured bobble hat
Dotted with bits of yellow straw.
You see I am a farmer's wife
With an early start each morning,
You'll often find me feeding calves
As the cold, crisp day is dawning.
Oh, yes, it's served me many years
This faithful woollen hat of mine,
Chewed on by hungry, dark-eyed calves
And moistened with frothy, white slime.
My hat pulled down around my ears
Keeps my head all warm and cosy,
The pom-pom bounces on the top
Like my cheeks, bright red and rosy.
Spattered with muck, I scrape the yard,
The aroma follows me round,
'Eau de bovine' perfumes my hat
From when it's been dropped on the ground.
I don't look like pin-up girl
With my bobble hat pulled on tight,
The pom-pom swaying on the top -
I imagine I'm quite a sight!
You may smile and make rude comments
About my scruffy attire,
But there's little point in dressing up
To wallow in muck and mire!

Owning a pedigree herd of Holstein Friesians meant that showing animals at local agricultural shows was often something we aspired to as was having them photographed for promotion purposes. Unfortunately, with the onslaught of TB it's not something we have been able to do for the past ten years or so due to restrictions on movements of animals but in those early days it was a common occurrence. I soon learnt a great deal about what constitutes a good cow. Initially I accused Tim of not feeding them enough as Holstein cattle are big, bony animals with protruding hip bones that you could hang your coat on - but he patiently explained that they are bred for maximum milk production and so not carrying surplus fat is a good sign as it means they are channelling their energy into producing milk and not meat! I learnt what traits to look for in a good cow; a straight top line, fluid locomotion, good udder conformation and depth of body to name but a few. I can remember on one occasion being sent to purchase a hair dryer for Tim to use when preparing the cows for showing. You can imagine the response I got when a helpful salesperson approached me in Boots while I was perusing the vast range of hairdryers and politely asked, "Are you looking for anything in particular? " I don't suppose it was every day that someone was looking for an appliance for a cow!

Getting ready for a show caused a buzz of excitement and meant an early start to the day. The selected animals had to be halter trained for days leading up to the event so that hopefully they behaved themselves in the show ring and didn't disgrace the handler who, more often than not, was Tim. The day before the show the cows were trimmed using clippers so that the udders were shown to their best advantage and their coats were sleek and shiny. On the morning itself they were washed and dried and then loaded onto a lorry along with all the necessary paraphernalia such as halters, brushes, shovels, buckets, food, straw bales for bedding and the display boards that proudly declared the exhibitor's name. Once at the show the cows would be tied into stands on a deep bed of clean straw, given a bucket of food to keep them happy and then watched like a hawk in case they lifted their tails. Should they show signs of emptying their bowels, someone would be at hand with a shovel to remove the offending muck so that they didn't lie in it and thereby compromise their chances of winning a rosette. For the duration of the show these bovine competitors could expect to be pampered prima-donnas before returning at the end of the day to the green fields of Withymoor Farm hopefully accompanied by shiny metal cups and official certificates emblazoned with our name.

The following poem was written as a response to a challenge given to me by a fifteen year-old boy in my church youth group many years ago. He knew I wrote poems and so set me the task of writing a poem which had to include the three elements of cows, football and our farm dog, Rebel. I wasn't sure if I would be able to meet the challenge but once I sat down and put pen to paper I started and couldn't stop thus making this the longest poem I have ever written!

WITHYLAND UNITED

There was once a dairy farmer who wasn't very bright,
He had a strange dream in the middle of the night;
He dreamt he'd become the manager of a team
Of football playing cows - the best there'd ever been.
He started on their training the very next day
But found that their udders got in the way.
They slowed them down immensely when they were full up
And looked as if they'd stop them from winning the cup.
Never to be beaten, the farmer scratched his head
And thought he'd make a corset for each cow instead,
To support their udders and stop them hanging down,
They really were the trimmest cows for miles around!
It soon became apparent that though they were keen,
Their defending skills were the worst he'd ever seen
So he substituted his farm dog as goalie,
A black and white collie by the name of Roly.
But, alas, poor old Roly was frightened of the ball
And dived out of sight if it came near him at all.
Then as a last resort, the farmer tried his pup,
So keen was he to win the Best Dairy Team Cup.
The puppy was called Rebel and fearless was he

As he took on the strikers single-handedly.
At football playing he was agile and adept
For not once did the ball slip past him to the net.
The success of the players soon made headline news
For every game they played they never seemed to lose,
Their faithful, doting fans cheered and got excited
So invincible were Withyland United!
They trained really hard, were disciplined and fit
And still wore their corsets as part of the kit,
Large transfer fees were offered but the coach declined
For the Dairy Cup Trophy was still on his mind.
After topping the League, the Cup Final Day came
But horror of horrors, a striker went down lame!
Another had mastitis in her back quarter
While a third caught TB and had to be slaughtered!
It seemed as though the cup was slipping from their hands
But they still played the game and made a valiant stand,
By the half-time whistle it was a one-all draw -
But could they score another? Their fans were not sure!
When the final whistle blew the score was unchanged
Which meant that penalties would have to be arranged,
The players were picked, you could feel the tension rise,
As Rebel stood his ground with calm and fearless eyes.
The penalties were taken, the crowd held its breath
As Rebel sprung to life and dived both right and left,
Intercepting every ball with lightening quick speed -
The canine goalie was a sight to watch indeed!
The Withyland strikers were nimble footed too,
Each time they kicked the ball, the goalie let it through.
The fans went wild as the farmer's eyes filled with tears
At the fulfilment of the dream he'd had for years.
So ends this saga of a bovine football team,
Probably the greatest the world has ever seen.
So don't dismiss your dreams as absurd or insane
For with hard work you too can climb the road to fame.

Chapter Eight

Jeremiah 6:16a (NLT)
This is what the Lord says:
"Stop at the crossroads and look around.
Ask for the old, godly way, and walk in it.
Travel its path, and you will find rest for your souls."

A Career Change

I continued to teach at Highnam Primary School and whilst enjoying the interaction with the children, found the mountain of paperwork and record-keeping less appealing. It seemed that the marking of books and preparing of lessons impinged more and more on my time in the evenings and at weekends and the infrequent appearance of OFSTED inspectors at the classroom doors just added to the pressure. Children were changing too it seemed. Highnam was a very middle class area where often both parents worked and the school's good reputation meant that academic expectations were high. I can remember on one occasion when two boys in my class were having a heated dispute, I threatened to "knock their heads together! " to which one of them responded, "I'll take you down for child abuse! " That single comment revealed to me the way things were changing and how, even at the age of ten, children were aware of their rights.

That having been said, I have lots of happy memories of teaching and I loved the kids but three years into our marriage my mind started exploring the possibility of a new venture. We had a lovely home with four good sized bedrooms and the added attraction of being on a farm - maybe, I tentatively suggested to Tim, I could run a B&B? Tim knew how much time I devoted to my job and how stressed I got at times as the government kept changing the goal posts with regards to the National Curriculum and Attainment Targets and so was fully supportive of a career change. We knew that the loss of my salary would be a big thing but on the other hand we were in the privileged position of not having a mortgage or rent to pay. After discussing the idea, we decided to give it a go and so during that final year of teaching the decorating began in earnest. Every half-term and school holiday would see me with a paint brush in hand critically appraising the house and preparing for the new venture. I handed in my resignation and shared with my class my plans for the future. I wrote a poem which I read to them and then set the challenge of a competition to illustrate it. The best one was chosen which depicted a Betty Boop-like character (me!) wearing wellies and carrying a bucket whilst shouting, "Come on Bessie, the guests need some milk for breakfast! " I had some post-cards printed with the illustrated poem on it and each child in my class was presented with one on my final day as a memento of our year together.

THE SCHOOLTEACHER
These lines of verse are based on me,
A lowly teacher – yes, that's me!
Led like a lamb to the slaughter each day
And shoved head-first into the classroom fray.
With unkind jokes about my hair
Like, 'Is there something lurking there?'
They will always argue that black is white,
And I'm always wrong while they're always right!
Gone are the days of fear and awe
When Teacher's word was like the law.
Respect was shown by obeying each word –
Something which pupils today find absurd!
So now it's time to say 'Goodbye',
And with relief I heave a sigh,

Leaving my life as a stressed-out teacher
To make Bed & Breakfast my new feature!

It was an emotional day as I said goodbye to staff members I had worked alongside for six years but I knew I would see them again as I had agreed to do some supply teaching while my new business got up and running. So ended one phase of my life and I looked forward with excited anticipation to what the next stage would bring!

I finished my full time teaching career at the end of the summer term in July 1997 and opened for business as a B&B proprietor on 1st August less than 2 weeks later. Looking back, I was very naive, but then I think the best way to learn is often by being thrown in at the deep end.

Our first paying guests were some friends of my parents from Kent. On the day they were due to arrive the new king size bed that we had ordered still hadn't been delivered and it was beginning to feel a bit like Fawlty Towers. Tim and I had a contingency plan that we would put our own bed in the B&B room and sleep on the floor ourselves if need be but thankfully a delivery van arrived late morning and the new bed was ensconced in the double room. I can still remember feeling very nervous that first week as I took orders and served up full English breakfasts each morning but soon got into the swing of it. The next awkwardness was presenting them with a bill at the end of their stay and that was an aspect of running a business that I struggled with for a long time as I hate asking people for money.

All in all things went pretty well for the first few months until a group of four young men arrived for a week. They worked for an advertising company that sold loyalty cards for pubs and were spending a week in the area promoting a local pub restaurant. They arrived straight from a previous job and so had lots of clothes that needed to be washed and were a bit disheartened to discover that the nearest launderette was six miles away in Ross-on-Wye. I don't usually offer a clothes washing service but since they were going to be staying for a week, I offered to do a couple of loads for them and they were delighted. After packing them off to work on a full cooked breakfast, I turned my attention to the washing and soon had a line full of colourful shirts blowing in the breeze. Sometime later I went to check on them and, discovering they still felt a bit damp, thought I'd put them to air on my mother-in-law's Aga in her kitchen as I had seen her do so often. Tim's mum was out when I popped next door and so I carefully folded the shirts in two piles on top of the Aga and returned next door to make beds and clean rooms.

A couple of hours later I returned to find the kitchen full of smoke and an acrid burning smell in the air which, on closer inspection was coming from the one pile of shirts! I was horrified. I had placed the shirts on top of the two dampers not realising that one was much hotter than the other and it was this one that had scorched the pile right through ruining four perfectly good shirts! What was I going to do? I grabbed both piles and rushed next door where I explained to Tim in a complete panic my misdemeanour showing him the still smouldering, scorched shirts as proof of my mishap. At that moment in time I simply wanted to run away and not have to explain to my guests how I had managed to ruin their shirts especially when peering at the labels I discovered names like Yves Saint Lauren and Armani - how was I ever going to replace them? I waited like a cat on hot bricks for their return that evening and once they were home I summoned up every ounce of courage and knocked on their bedroom door holding the burnt-smelling shirts as evidence. As the door was opened I launched into a garbled explanation beginning with the words, "I've had a bit of an accident! " and ending with the promise to replace the shirts with brand new ones the very next day. The young men seemed rather bemused by my evident discomfort and suggested that I "Chill out and have a beer! " They really weren't too bothered at all and found the whole thing rather amusing. When I pointed out that I had ruined some very expensive shirts they looked a bit confused but as I jabbed my finger at the Yves Saint Laurent label the penny dropped and they smiled even more as they admitted to having bought them in a charity shop. I returned downstairs feeling very much relieved and if I had had a beer in the house I might just have taken their advice and sat down to chill with one. The next day after breakfast I made my way into Gloucester where I bought 4 new shirts in Debenhams (their own brand) and waved goodbye to my profit from that particular booking whilst silently vowing never to do guests' laundry again.

That was the first of my Basil Fawlty experiences of which over the next 16 years there were many more. This is partly the inspiration for writing this book as my sister-in-law Helen thought it would make good reading!

There was the time when the telephone rang and a very posh female voice asked if I had a twin room for herself and a friend for two nights in a couple of months' time. She went to great lengths to tell me that they usually stayed in expensive hotels but wanted to do the whole B&B experience as a change. As I booked her in and put down the receiver I was left wondering why on earth they had chosen my establishment for their virgin voyage into the delights of farmhouse B&B? At about that time a farming friend was in the throes of lambing and he phoned up one day to say he had three orphan lambs and would I be interested in rearing them? The challenge appealed to me so he brought them over in the back of his pick-up and I made a pen with electric fencing on them back lawn with an old dog kennel in the middle for them to sleep in and so it was that Milly, Molly and Mandy joined our family. They were delightful and I loved watching them playing and jumping about in their enclosure. I bought some bottle teats and milk powder from Countrywide and got into the rhythm of feeding them three or four times a day. As soon as I appeared with the bottles of milk I was stampeded as I straddled the electric fence wire and soon perfected the art of holding a bottle in each hand while gripping the third one tightly between my knees ensuring they could all feed at the same time. I felt like a proper farmer's wife and my three woolly charges grew steadily as the weeks passed.

One morning as I came down into the kitchen, I glanced across at the lamb's pen to discover it was empty - they had managed to break through the electric fence! I rushed outside into the garden and you can imagine my horror when I espied them next door on my mother-in-law's patio happily munching through her beautiful flower pots and looking very contented. I shooed them off the patio and managed to persuade them to go back in their pen using food as the bargaining chip but knew that now they had a taste of freedom, it wouldn't be long before they attempted another jail break. Something had to be done. As it happened there was an empty shed in the corner of the farmyard and it seemed the ideal place to keep them as they were due to be picked up anytime soon by the farmer friend to go and join the rest of his sheep.

That afternoon I donned my wellies and decided to transfer my three lambs to their new residence - surely it couldn't be that difficult? I disconnected the electric fence and made an opening, all the while calling to them and walking confidently towards the farmyard. They were used to my voice and so happily followed me as I passed through the garden gate, excitedly running behind me like ducklings behind a mother duck. That's where the similarity ended because once in the open space of the farmyard with lots of new things to see, they bolted off in all directions not sure which way to explore first! I gathered my wits and tried not to let panic overtake me as I had visions of them galloping off down the road never to be seen again. I headed at a jog towards the door of the shed where I wanted them to go and grabbed a bucket that I had placed inside with food in and shook it noisily while waving it at them. This had the desired effect of stopping them in their tracks and I had their attention again. Calling their names I moved closer to them so they could see the food in the bucket and as they came running towards me I backed towards the door with them in hot pursuit. They hesitated at the door but thankfully the temptation of food was too great and they stepped over the threshold as I sprinkled the contents of the bucket on the ground. As they munched hungrily I quietly slipped behind them and shut the door - mission accomplished!

Hearing the purr of an engine, I looked up to see an immaculate, black BMW roll into the yard and pull up in front of the house. As I watched, two equally immaculate ladies stepped out and looked around them, taking in their surroundings with a somewhat alarmed expression. They were well dressed, hair beautifully coiffured and looked completely out of place in the middle of a working farmyard. It was at this point that I realised my B&B guests had arrived, somewhat earlier than expected, and that I needed to introduce myself. I hurriedly wiped my grubby hands on my jeans and made my way towards them looking hot and flustered whilst trying to muster a welcoming smile. On reaching the car, I introduced myself as the person they had spoken to when they made the reservation and suggested that they go on inside and I would be there in a moment or two to show them to their room. As they took in my Wellington boots, scruffy work clothes and generally dishevelled look, I could see them both wondering what exactly they had come to. While they extracted their cases from the boot of the BMW I ran around to the back of the house, pulled off my wellies and washed my hands so I looked a little more presentable by the time they entered through the front door. I showed them up to their room, suggested places where they could get an evening meal and made polite conversation to get things onto a better footing. They seemed pleased with the standard of the room and started to explain that the purpose of their visit was to try and find an outfit for a wedding later that summer as of the one ladies was mother of the bride. It transpired they had been shopping in London and Bath but to no avail and so had decided to give Malvern a try. I tried not to look too shocked when they announced that they didn't want anything too extravagant and weren't looking to spend more than £1,000! It crossed my mind again at this point that they would have been far better suited to a five star hotel rather than my humble establishment but they settled themselves in and then set off later to find a local hostelry where they could enjoy a meal.

The following day I was responsible for preparing a craft activity for the Mother and Toddler group I helped run at the church in Newent and so I gathered my bits and pieces and settled myself down on the floor of the lounge with a pair of scissors and the paper flower petal shapes I needed to cut out. Sometime later I was still engrossed in this task as I heard the front door open and the two ladies return from their meal. I assumed they would make their way to their room to retire for the evening but to my surprise the lounge door was flung open (totally ignoring the 'Private' sign on it) and they peered down at me with great interest and said in their posh voices, “Oh, what are you doing? “ I explained my task and they seemed very intrigued and asked, “Oh, can we help? “ Before I had the chance to reply they delved into their handbags, fished out a pair of nail scissors, plonked themselves down on either end of the sofa and set to with gusto cutting out daffodil petals. It certainly speeded up the process and left me very bemused that these two well-to-do ladies could get so much enjoyment out of a simple task! They certainly embraced the whole B&B experience and I hope it left a positive impression on their memories - they definitely did on mine. Oh, and by the way, they did manage to find a suitable wedding outfit in Malvern but I didn’t dare enquire how much it set them back!

Chapter Nine

Psalm 50:10 (NLT)
For all the animals of the forest are mine,
and I own the cattle on a thousand hills.

Down on the Farm

As I mentioned previously I had always dreamt of being a farmer's wife and so over the years I have found myself up close and personal with some of the farm residents. One memorable occasion started off with my usual excursion to do the weekly food shop at the local supermarket in Ross-on-Wye. Having wrestled in the aisles with the throngs, filled my trolley and made my purchases, I set off for home. I pulled into the farmyard, parked outside the front door and then proceeded to carry bags of shopping from the boot of the car, in through the front door, down the hallway and into the kitchen where I deposited them on the table ready for unpacking and putting into cupboards. My mind was totally focussed on the task in hand as I marched to and fro and I was completely oblivious of my name being called frantically by Tim who was outside in the farmyard. You can imagine my surprise when, after depositing a few more bags of shopping on the kitchen table, I turned to find myself eye-ball to eye-ball with a fully grown cow stood in my kitchen doorway! I don't know who was more surprised - me or her!

Tim had been bringing her up from one end of the farm to the other and he said she saw me walking into the house and just took off after me. He tried yelling to warn me but I hadn't heard his shouts and so now I was left with a bit of a problem as I had a 3/4 tonne cow to deal with in my hallway! Tim was stood outside the front door imagining the chaos that was about to ensue as the cow got spooked and tried to turn around to escape. He had visions of her redecorating the walls and floor with muck (that's the first thing they do when stressed!) and taking the stairs and door frame with her as she tried to turn because cows don't like reversing! Thankfully I was unaware of the potential destruction and did the first thing that came into my mind. I walked slowly towards her while talking gently and suggesting that she might be better going back outside as it was a bit cramped for her in the house. She obligingly started reversing quietly back down the length of the hallway and neatly out through the front door much to Tim's utter amazement. There was no muck splattered everywhere and no damage done - no-one would have known that a cow had just been stood in my kitchen doorway moments before! I think in that moment I went up in my husband's estimation and my skills as a cow-whisperer were birthed.

Our herd of pedigree Holstein Friesians have been built up over a period of 65 years since Tim's dad first bought the farm in 1950. Breeding and blood lines are very important and Tim and his brother Ian have both trained to do artificial inseminating so that we can use semen from the best bulls across the world. The gestation period for a cow is 9 months and generally they just get on and calve without too much difficulty but of course there are always exceptions. On one occasion a cow was having a hard time in labour and Tim knew something was wrong and that a vet was needed.

When the vet arrived and assessed the situation he said he would have to do a Caesarean. For this the cow is given a local anaesthetic and while she is standing an incision is made down her side and the calf is pulled out. All went to plan until it came to the point when Nick, the vet, had to sew up the incision he had made and the cow simply would not stand still. Between them the vet and Tim tried to keep the new mother stationary while he finished the task but she was having none of it and although her head was tethered, she kept swinging her body around from side to side getting more and more agitated. Obviously the longer the incision was open, the greater the chance of infection so it was important to get the job done as quickly as possible.

The first thing I knew about these proceedings was when the telephone rang in the house and Tim requested that I come and talk to a cow please! I pulled on my wellies and hurried off down the yard to the maternity wing where I discovered that Nick had requested my services to try and calm the stressed animal. I immediately went and stood at her head, stroking her ears and talking in a low, soothing voice. What do you talk to a cow about? I can't remember exactly what I said and I don't suppose it matters much but it had the desired effect of calming her so that she stood still and Nick could finish the stitching. Tim used this as sermon illustration the following Sunday morning and it inspired Kath Smith, a member of the congregation and my Bible Study group, to write this poem which I have included with her permission.

THE COW WHISPERER

Katrina was in her kitchen. Tim was down on the farm.
The telephone rang at the farmhouse, its shrill message filled with alarm.
"I need you, " said Tim - he seemed worried, "Can you manage to get here somehow?
Just leave all your housework and come down. I need you to talk to the cow! "
Katrina raced down to the big shed. The cow was in labour she knew.
"It must be important, " she thought, but just what would they want her to do?
What words could she say to the poor cow? Just what would the cow want to hear?
When she entered the shed she could see that the cow was in turbulent fear!
The vet had performed a Caesarean and the calf had been born safe and well
But they needed the mother to keep still - they were having a

job she could tell.
Katrina put hands round the cow's head, then moved her face close to its ear,
She whispered some comforting words which she hoped would alleviate fear.
Just what did she whisper I wonder? Did she say, " It's all right I am here.
I will stay 'till it's over my dear friend, it will soon be all right never fear.
You will soon be back out in the fresh fields, with your little calf prancing around -
Just think of those sweet-smelling grasses, so green as they cover the ground.
This darkness and dread will be over and you will be free from all pain,
The sun will come out on the meadow and banish the frost and the rain.
The air will be full of a new life - your child will be there firm and strong -
You will teach him to feed and be happy and the world will be like a new song!"

I love seeing calves born and I never tire of the wonder of new life and how quickly these little creatures are up on their spindly legs looking for milk. Expectant mothers are housed together in a straw barn and Tim and his brother Stephen take it in turns alternate nights to check on them and make sure none of them are calving as sometimes they need help. One night I had retired to bed as Tim went out to check the maternity wing but several minutes later he was stood in the bedroom door asking if I would please get dressed again because a heifer was calving and he thought she would need some help.

Until a cow has had two calves, she is called a heifer and sometimes these young cows will have problems giving birth especially if the calf is a large one. By the time they have had three of four calves they are old hands at it and don't often need assistance. For those that need a helping hand a tool called a calving aid is used. This medieval-looking contraption consists of a metal bar in a U-shape with another longer bar attached at an angle of 90 degrees. The whole thing is nearly 2m in length. The U-shaped part sits on the back of the cow under the tail with the two ends resting on her hips. There are two hooks on each prong where a rope can be attached and then the other end of the rope is tied around the calves' feet inside the cow. When the cow pushes, there is a winch on the handle of the calving aid (the equivalent of 3 men pulling) which is used to pull at the same time thereby speeding up the process. Sometimes if a cow takes too long calving the calf will die before it's born and so the calving aid improves the success rate of live calves even though when I first saw it I thought it looked more like an instrument of torture!

On this occasion when I arrived in the barn suitably attired in old clothes and wellies, Tim had the calving aid at the ready and we managed between us to manoeuvre the somewhat sparky heifer into a corner where he managed to fit the aid onto her hips. She lulled us into a false sense of security and seemed to be settling down when all of a sudden she whipped around unexpectedly and the long 2m metal handle swung with her. I didn't move quickly enough and the end of the metal handle caught me well and truly on my jaw causing a shooting pain which brought me to my knees in the straw, clutching my face. Tim looked horror-struck as I brought my hand away to see what the damage was and there was blood trickling down my chin. It looked worse than it was though and a quick examination revealed no broken teeth, just a cut lip and a bruised jaw much to our relief. Once I'd pulled myself together and the initial pain had subsided we returned to the job of calving the miscreant cow but this time I was better prepared to move quickly if circumstances dictated. As it happens everything went smoothly and we were able to get the job done quickly and leave mother and baby to get acquainted. As Tim has since commented, we had to make sure the calf was born alive even at the expense of a nearly decapitated wife! It's just as well I understand where my place is in his affections - his beloved cows will always take priority although since that occasion I have demanded he pay me danger money if he requires my assistance with calving!

As numbers of livestock farms in this country diminish, vets have less and less experience of treating large animals. We have used the same veterinary practice since 1950 and when Nick retired from the practice three years ago numbers of dairy farms on their books had dropped to just fifteen. Today there are just five including ours. Nick was always wanting to learn and to try new things and so once when a calf was born with internal complications and wasn't expected to live, he asked if he might try and operate to see if he could save her although he wasn't too optimistic. He duly carried out the surgery and then little Lilac was put in a shed across the farmyard under a heat lamp to see if she would recover.

She was a very poorly little calf and I used to go out several times a day to check on her but things didn't look too promising as she wasn't eating or drinking. I tried tempting her with various things but she just wasn't interested - it looked like Nick's prognosis was going to be correct. However, the more time I spent with this little calf, the more attached I got and the more determined to help her recover. For the first time ever I sat on a bale of straw alongside her, put my hands on her back and prayed that God would heal her - my first prayer of healing for an animal. I then had an idea. I had tried tempting her with grass, silage and calf nuts all to no avail but now I tried porridge. I made some porridge with milk and stirred in a couple of teaspoons of honey to sweeten it and took it out to my patient. I sat on the bale next to her, scooped some porridge onto my fingers and let her sniff at it, talking all the while and imploring her to eat some. She sniffed at it very unenthusiastically but put her long, rough tongue out to taste it. I held my breath. She tried a bit more. It seemed to have her interest now and so I scooped some more onto my hand. A few more mouthfuls and it was gone so I let her eat it straight out of the container until it was licked clean. It was the first time she had eaten in days and this was the turning point in her recovery. From then on I would make a dish of porridge a couple of times a day and take it out to her and she would polish it off and look for more.

She looked like a different animal within days - her eyes were bright, she would stand at the half-door looking out for my arrival and the wound from the surgery was healing nicely. I soon had her eating calf nuts and straw and drinking water as her appetite grew and grew. When Nick the vet returned to deal with another animal a fortnight later, he asked my brother-in-law about the calf he had operated on, not expecting her to be alive. Ian said he had something to show him. He led Nick over to Lilac's shed and there was the calf looking fit and healthy much to Nick's surprise and his surprise increased when Ian told him the story and concluded, "It's the power of porridge and prayer! " That no doubt gave him something to think about!

Not all such stories have happy endings however. On other occasions the patients haven't pulled through despite lots of loving care and attention. Cherry was a little white heifer calf who had lost form over a period of weeks and so was put into a shed on her own where her eating could be monitored closely and where she was less susceptible to picking up infections from the other calves. She seemed to do well initially and her eating improved but suddenly she took a turn for the worse and quietly wasted away despite medical intervention from the vet and TLC from me. I would sit out in the straw with her head cradled in my lap and talk to her and stroke her and I sobbed my heart out on the morning I found her dead. Farming is a tough way of life which teaches resilience and endurance. The cows have to be milked three times a day even on Christmas Day and New Year's Day. Regardless of the weather conditions Mother Nature decides to throw at you be it freezing, horizontal rain, buffeting winds or blistering heat, the cows have to be fed and the calves tended to. Farmers are a hardy breed who are used to long working hours and hard manual labour. I know of some dairy farmers who have not taken a holiday in decades because they can't afford to pay someone to come and milk the cows in their absence. Death of livestock, breakdowns in machinery, frozen water pipes, failed crops and poor financial returns are all things which are sent to try farmers and yet I can see how this was all part of our training ground for pastoring a church as resilience is a necessary requirement.

Having a herd of 160 dairy cows that need to be milked three times a day keeps everyone busy and anything that speeds up that process is embraced. It is for that reason that we have always had dogs on the farm so that they can be used to bring the cows in from the fields for milking. Our latest canine helper is called Max and I bought him as a puppy from a local farm. He was the fattest of the litter and the most inquisitive so I chose him and collected him when he was old enough to leave his mother. Max is a working dog and as such is not allowed in the house - can you imagine the state of my floors and carpets if he were allowed in after running through yards inches deep in cow muck? It doesn't bear thinking about! Anyway, right from the start it was my job to walk him and train him so I enrolled him for Puppy Training classes at the local village hall.

Now, up until this point I had been taking Max for walks each day around the fields on the farm and he was used to running ahead to explore hedgerows and exciting scents. When I took him to Puppy Training classes I was asked to put him on a lead so that he learnt not to pull and so I would have more control over him. I managed to borrow an old lead off one of the other people at the class and clipped it onto his collar. The first task we were asked to do was to walk around the circle with our puppy on a lead and allow them to meet and greet every other puppy and owner. When it came to our turn I called Max and started off confidently around the circle but to my utter embarrassment he refused to stand up in silent protest to the restriction of the lead. I was determined not to be dictated to by my wayward charge and so dragged him on his bottom across the slippery wooden floor around the circle to meet the other puppies but he stubbornly refused to participate much to the amusement of the other owners! For the rest of the evening we sat and watched as they were put through their paces but Max was having none of it - even ignoring the lure of doggy treats. Following our disastrous first lesson, I took him out for walks on the lead a few times during the week and thankfully by the next class he redeemed himself and behaved admirably - he was a quick learner.

We attended regularly for 9 weeks and during that time Max mastered simple commands like "sit ", "stay " and "come " and also learnt social skills which meant he could interact well with other dogs and their owners. After a shaky start all was well and I was glad I had persevered.

At about this time Tim decided to train him to run alongside him on his early morning jog which he aimed to do a couple of times a week. He found a piece of baling string and tied one end to Max's collar and the other end to a belt loop on his shorts and off they went. Sometime later I happened to be looking out of the window as Tim reappeared in the farmyard holding onto his shorts, the string and Max. It transpired that things had been going smoothly until Max had caught sight of a cat and had darted off after it giving rise to a tearing sound as Tim's shorts ripped under the tension and were in danger of ending up around his ankles unless he took swift action! He had then been forced to finish his run hanging onto the waistband of his shorts at the same time as holding onto the string. As you can imagine this was not conducive to a smooth and elegant running technique and somewhat cramped his style! However, Tim is nothing if not tenacious and he refused to let this little set-back faze him. The next time he went for his early morning jog, he buckled a leather belt around his waist and tied Max to this so if there should be a repetition of former events his shorts wouldn't be compromised. It wasn't long before Max had learnt to run alongside him on this three mile route and not to allow himself to be distracted. He even jumps up onto the grass verge and lies flat if a car passes on the road – the only problem with this is that it interrupts Tim's running rhythm especially as he often hears the cars long before he sees them!

Chapter Ten

Hebrews13:2 (NLT)
Don't forget to show hospitality to strangers, for some who have done this have entertained angels without realizing it!

B&B Bloomers

Our congregation knows how much Tim's cows mean to him as he often refers to them in his sermons and over the years various church members have bought him cow paraphernalia to adorn his office and our home. He has been given canvas prints, egg cups, cross-stitch pictures, pen holders, a cookery apron, ornaments, door stops, cuddly toys and a whole host of other items on the cow theme and whilst I am very fond of cows too, I have had to put my foot down or else the house would look like a cow museum! Having said that, in the sixteen years that I ran a Bed & Breakfast business in the farmhouse, I always advertised as a "Working Dairy Farm " so that people had a clear idea of what they were coming too.

Just up the road from the farm in the next village of Gorsley is a thriving Baptist church which until recently hosted an annual flower festival over the August Bank Holiday. It started off as a small affair but over the years it gathered momentum as word spread and each August the narrow country lanes would be bustling with cars and coaches as visitors arrived in droves to see the spectacular flower displays in the main church hall and to hear great Bible teaching from speakers such as Tony Campolo, Jeff Lucas and Charles Price.

Being the nearest B&B to the church meant that my rooms were always in demand for the Bank Holiday weekend and I could have booked the 2 bedrooms out at least 5 times over! For many years I had a lovely family from Worcester book into the family room and another retired missionary from Nepal would reserve the twin room and would bring a different friend with her each year. This was the case for many years until on one occasion the missionary lady was recovering from surgery and so was unable to come, leaving the room available for someone else to reserve. It wasn't long before the phone rang and a retired Baptist minister and his wife booked the room for the duration of the weekend.

When the Bank Holiday arrived the family from Worcester greeted us like long lost friends and settled into their room on the Friday evening and then the doorbell rang and the other couple introduced themselves. My first thought was that the wife was very reminiscent of Hyacinth Bucket from the TV series "Keeping up Appearances ", and this proved to be an accurate appraisal. It was a hot summer's evening and all the windows were open in order to encourage a flow of air through the house. I showed the new couple up to their en-suite room and then after explaining about breakfast and pointing out the hospitality tray in their room, I left them to settle in and retired back downstairs to the kitchen. It was only about 2 minutes later that the bedroom door was flung open and 'Hyacinth ' staggered down the stairs flapping her hands in front of her grimacing face and exclaiming, "Oh the smell, the smell! " She said the farm smell in the room was overpowering and could she have some air freshener to get rid of it! I duly gave her a can of air freshener and she hurried back up the stairs, shut all the windows in the stifling hot room and commenced to spray lavender breeze lavishly around the room. I must confess I found the whole thing very amusing although I did feel a pang of compassion for her hapless husband. For the rest of the weekend anyone passing their bedroom door would hear the hiss of the aerosol spray at regular intervals and if you were unfortunate enough to be walking by when the door was opened you were assailed by the fumes of lavender breeze which hit the back of your throat and made your eyes water! At breakfast the next morning I heard Hyacinth bemoaning the terrible aroma of the farm before beating a hasty retreat back up the stairs to the sanctuary of her room leaving the other guests in fits of helpless laughter around the table. Needless to say Mr & Mrs Bucket didn't book in again the following year!

Another time, over the May Bank Holiday weekend when there was a special event on at Gorsley Baptist Church, we had a lady called Mrs Cox book in for three nights. My in-laws were amenable to me using what was technically one of their bedrooms which had access from both sides of the house, theirs and ours. The room wasn't en-suite which meant that the incumbent would have to share the main bathroom with Tim and myself. It was into this room that I booked Mrs Cox as the other two en-suite rooms had already been reserved. When Mrs. Cox arrived she proved to be a warm, friendly woman who was very down to earth as she chatted away to us and the other guests. She asked me for some advice on where she might go for an early morning run before breakfast so I directed her around some of the country lanes and subsequently each morning before breakfast she would do a 3 mile circuit. She wasn't a young woman, I estimated she was in her 60s, and so I was suitably impressed by both her discipline and stamina. We didn't see much of her over the three days while she was attending the special event but when we did have the opportunity to interact with her she was very pleasant and unassuming and seemed appreciative of her accommodation.

On the final morning, as she stood in the hallway with her bags packed, I asked her to sign the visitors' book and was surprised to see her write; Baroness Caroline Cox, House of Lords, House of the Lord. Unbeknown to us we had been hosts to the Deputy Speaker in the House of Lords, a lady with a strong Christian faith who is a renowned human rights campaigner in places such as Sudan, Burma and Russia. She told us she tried to keep fit by jogging as on more than one occasion she had literally had to run for her life when danger threatened. Before she left she invited us to London and said she would very much enjoy showing us around the House of Lords if we so desired and the following week her autobiography arrived in the post with a personal message handwritten inside the fly leaf thanking us for our "splendid hospitality and Christian ministry ". We both thoroughly enjoyed reading her book and it just served to prove to us what a formidable and yet humble woman she is and how her faith is central to her life as she seeks to be a voice for the voiceless. We certainly felt honoured to have had her in our home.

As I read her book and pondered on the many people her life has touched and transformed, it made me think of Jesus. He came to set prisoners free, to bring hope to those in darkness and despair. Baroness Cox may have changed the course of people's lives while they were here on earth but Jesus' love and compassion changed lives for eternity by paying a debt no-one else could. This thought inspired the following poem:

SUCH LOVE

Never my sweet Jesus will I fully understand
Why you let the soldiers hammer nails into your hand –
Why you took the whipping, the crown of thorns on your head
When you had the power to call angels down instead;
They were poised for your command in heaven up above
Instead you took the punishment, so great was your love.
Hell unleashed its fury, in the crowd Satan looked on,
Innocence was crucified for you had done no wrong.
You chose to bear the pain, the scorn and the derision
For since the birth of the world this was your decision –
You planted 'choice' in our hearts, we chose to go astray
The things of this world were more enticing than your way.
You watched us fall and stumble, tears glistened in your eyes
As we were taken in by the Devil's silky lies.
Then in your perfect timing, from heaven you stepped down
To be born in a cattle shed in a sleepy town;
Mighty King of heaven in a baby's tiny form
Nestled in a manger, so vulnerable and forlorn.
Half a life-time later, that baby is now a man
And we see the fulfilment of your redemptive plan;
The mighty king of heaven hung on a cross of wood

Taking all my guilt and shame, dying to make me good
Purchasing my salvation and a place up above
While I'm left to marvel at the power of such love.

Late one evening I locked the doors, turned off the lights and was heading up the stairs to bed when the doorbell rang. This was a rather unusual occurrence at 10pm and so on opening the door I was surprised to find a couple stood on the doorstep smiling expectantly at me. I smiled back and asked if I could help them at which point they seemed a little taken aback and said that they had a room reserved. Now it was my turn to look surprised. I told them that I was pretty sure they didn't have a booking as I had checked the diary earlier and didn't have any reservations for that evening and so hadn't been expecting them. However, just to prove my point I picked the diary up off the side and invited them in for a moment while I flipped to the relevant date. You can imagine my horror when there on the page it stated quite clearly that the couple had booked in for one night and would be arriving late. I couldn't believe my eyes and could only assume that when I had checked the diary earlier in the day I had inadvertently looked at the wrong page!

I apologised profusely and explained that I needed to get the room ready for them which would only take me 10-15 minutes. In the meantime I called Tim and asked him to make a pot of tea and entertain our new arrivals in the dining room. I ran up the stairs like a woman possessed clutching the vacuum cleaner in one hand and a duster in the other and set to getting the king-size bed made, the en-suite bathroom cleaned and the bedroom dusted and vacuumed. Once everything was completed about 15 minutes later I returned downstairs where Tim was dutifully entertaining our guests by talking animatedly about the farm. I smiled sweetly at the lady and asked if she wanted to come up and see the room before carrying the bags up.

Our double room is spacious and airy with fresh, modern decor and co-ordinated soft furnishings and most guests are delighted with the room especially when they see the view across to May Hill.

However, as soon as the lady set foot in the room I sensed something was wrong. I did my usual spiel about the hospitality trays, heating controls and breakfast arrangements but it was obvious from her discomfort that something was amiss. In the end I decided to take the bull by the horns so to speak and asked if there was something wrong with the room. At this she shook her head and said that the room was lovely but they had requested a twin room as they were not husband and wife as I had assumed, but rather brother and sister and consequently wanted 2 single beds and not a king-size one. As the proverbial penny dropped, I plastered a smile back on my face and suggested that she return back downstairs for another cup of tea while I got the twin room ready!

So it was action replay as I ran back up the stairs again with the Hoover and left Tim to regale his captive audience with more farming tales as I got the twin room ready, all the while comparing myself to Basil Fawlty and wishing I had a Manuel to call upon. Finally, another 15 minutes later and looking decidedly hot and flustered, I was able to usher our guests up to their room and finally climb into bed myself feeling quite exhausted while Tim found the whole incident very amusing. Breakfast the following morning was uneventful and they left shortly afterwards saying they had very much enjoyed their stay of which I was doubtful after the fiasco of the previous evening. However, I can only assume they were genuine in their praise as the following week they phoned up again to book a night's stay on their return journey but unfortunately that night we were already fully booked. Some people are just gluttons for punishment!

Chapter Eleven

Isaiah 43:18-20 (NLT)
"But forget all that—
it is nothing compared to what I am going to do.
For I am about to do something new.
See, I have already begun! Do you not see it?
I will make a pathway through the wilderness."

A New Thing!

In April 2003, having been happily married to a farmer for over 10 years, I felt a growing consternation as Tim started talking about how he felt God was nudging him in a different direction - possibly into part-time Christian ministry. To be honest I put it down to him having a mid-life crisis as he approached his 40th birthday in October and so carried on with life thinking it would all blow over. I was very happy serving in our church in Newent; working with the youth, helping with the mother & toddler group and teaching a Sunday School class. Tim and I headed up a Homegroup together, he delivered the occasional Sunday message and we hosted the young people's Afterchurch periodically on a Sunday evening. Life was good and I saw no reason to change anything but God had different ideas.

Leading up to his birthday Tim felt increasingly that he needed to step back from the farm and get involved in some part-time Christian ministry but he knew very definitely that it needed to be linked to the local church which he believes passionately is the power house of Christian growth and maturity. The church in

Newent which he had grown up in already had several family members in positions of leadership; his father was an elder and his two brothers were youth leaders and so it was difficult to see how he could use his gifts on a regular basis within the church without causing a Cracknell overload.

For some years the leadership at Glebe Chapel, Newent had been involved in running a Sunday afternoon service at the little Gospel Hall in Station Street, Cinderford. This small fellowship consisted of one young family plus a handful of elderly ladies who were determined to keep the doors open as a Christian witness to the town but it was becoming more difficult as the elderly ladies became increasingly frail. The church elders at Newent had approached an organisation called CPI (Church Planting Initiative) who they hoped would be able to find a young couple willing to head up the dying Gospel Hall and give it a new lease of life but as yet no headway had been made. Over a period of months Tim prayed for clarification from God as to what he should be doing and as he did so the name "Cinderford " kept coming into his mind. This wasn't what he was expecting and so he ignored it for a while in the hope God's calling was to somewhere more exciting than an old mining town in the depths of the Forest of Dean. However the name kept intruding onto his consciousness but he didn't share his thoughts with anyone except me so no-one else knew that a change was in the offing.

On his 40th birthday a verse handwritten inside the card from his parents read;

> Acts 20:24 (NLT)
> But my life is worth nothing to me unless I use it for finishing the work assigned me by the Lord Jesus—the work of telling others the Good News about the wonderful grace of God.

His mum had chosen the verse not knowing anything about the stirrings within Tim's heart and totally unaware of how timely this was but for Tim it was the first of several confirmations that gave him the confidence to move forwards. Sometime after his birthday he told me that he felt sure that God was calling us to get involved in pastoring the old Gospel Hall in Cinderford. To say I was not impressed with this revelation is an understatement. I was not happy with God. Why was he having this conversation with Tim and not me? Why did I not feel any nudgings or promptings to step out in faith? What if Tim wasn't hearing things clearly and had got it wrong? I felt my gifts were being used quite adequately at Glebe Chapel where I had lots of good friends and I felt fulfilled. Why would God ask me to leave this and move to a church where I knew no-one and where there were no youth for me to work with? What was he thinking?

As you can I imagine I had quite a few candid conversations with God during this time of transition and even considered digging my heels in and refusing to move. I knew of another Christian couple who worshipped in different churches and so I thought we could do the same - I'd stay at Newent and Tim could go to Cinderford. However, once I'd stamped my foot, and recovered from my fit of pique, I realised that God would not want us in separate churches and I resigned myself to following my husband on this new journey. However, I didn't do it very graciously and it certainly wasn't with a sense of anticipation or excitement.

In hindsight I think I was scared. I had loved being a farmer's wife and felt well suited to the role, but a pastor's wife? That was a different thing altogether. My mind flipped back to nights of drunken excess during my college years and I couldn't equate my behaviour then with being a pastor's wife. Surely God had got the wrong woman? What would people think about me if they found out? What if I wasn't spiritual enough? I felt like a fraud and it wasn't a nice feeling. I really didn't think I was cut out for this new role at all so concluded that God had better do something drastic like giving me an intravenous shot of holiness or godly wisdom to help me meet people's expectations and overcome my own deep misgivings. I certainly struggled to remind myself of the fact that God’s grace is sufficient for me and that his power is made perfect in weakness (2 Corinthians 12:9)

SAVING GRACE
Drops of sweat like blood dripped down
Into the thirsty earth,
In the garden's peaceful calm
Your anguished soul gave birth
To cries of such agony
That Heaven's angels wept
While drugged by weariness
Your three disciples slept.
There in dark Gethsemane
You pleaded with your Lord
That you might be spared the pain
And to Heaven be restored,
But after this you added,
"Your will not mine be done! "
And so a loving Father
Offered His only Son.
You walked the road to Calvary
Knowing what lay ahead,
And on that cross hewn from wood
Your crimson blood was shed
To redeem the human race
From its evil and sin,
And to let God's saving grace
Like a flood tide rush in.

Tim was invited to speak at the Christmas Day service at Glebe Chapel that year and he prayed that God would give him another sign that pastoring a church and stepping back from the farm business was indeed the right thing. He gave his message and waited. There was no obvious response to the Gospel message which he was quietly hoping for but as he was chatting to various people afterwards a lovely Christian lady who we knew well walked by and stated in quite a matter of fact way, "Well, I don't think you'll be doing farming for much longer! " With that she walked off leaving Tim staring open-mouthed after her. It was a clear indication that it was time to step out in faith and respond to God's promptings.

Following this we took tentative steps forwards by meeting up with the couple who had been the mainstay in keeping the church in Cinderford ticking over until fresh troops arrived. We were invited to their home and had a time of prayer together as we sought God's will and his plans and purposes for us as a couple. It was during his quiet time the following morning that Tim read these verses in Isaiah 43:18-20 (NLT)

"But forget all that—
  it is nothing compared to what I am going to do.
For I am about to do something new.
  See, I have already begun! Do you not see it?
I will make a pathway through the wilderness."

This struck him forcibly. Tim felt God was saying that he was planning to do a new thing in Cinderford, he was going to make a pathway in the Forest for people to find him. This verse, after the previous night's prayer time, was the confirmation that Cinderford was where God was calling us to. It was the final piece in the jigsaw puzzle and ushered us forwards into pursuing things more formally. We had our first interview with Counties, one of the partner organisations which formed CPI, in September 2004 followed by a second one in November with CPI before we were officially taken on as CPI workers in Cinderford. We used the first few months in our new role to visit various growing churches around the UK to try and glean tips and wisdom on successful church growth. Also in February 2005, once we had the all-clear from TB, we had a big sale on the farm. The top 100 cows were sold, thereby reducing the amount of work to be done in readiness for Tim taking more of a back seat with regards to the day to day running of the farm business. One evening in March 2005 we had a special service at our church in Newent to commend us to the new work in Cinderford and Tim then started working 3 days a week in the church and 3 days on the farm. He was now officially a pastor and I was a pastor's wife, albeit a reluctant one.

To begin with our new church consisted of just a handful of old ladies and one family with three young children. This was the nucleus that we were going to build on and to kick start things off we had help from a group of students who came on a placement from a Bible College in Motherwell, Scotland. They were an energetic group and were willing to roll up their sleeves and get stuck in. Tim designed a questionnaire about the role of church in the community and armed with this the students went out around the town of Cinderford knocking on doors and asking people for their opinions. The results from the 150-200 people who took part were then correlated and this helped us to make informed choices about how the church might meet these perceived needs in the local community.

We also did several outreach events organised by the students such as a quiz evening and an Indian meal to encourage new people to come and meet us and to raise the profile of the church. One of the things suggested on the questionnaires was to change the time of the service from 3pm on a Sunday afternoon to 10.30am on a Sunday morning as the vast majority of people questioned had stated this as their preferred time for a church service. This caused great consternation among the half a dozen elderly ladies as they had been persuading their friends from other churches in the town to join us for the afternoon service but by changing it to the morning this would mean the friends wouldn't be able to come as they would have their own church services to attend.

However, we forged ahead with the time change and actually found that a few new people came along so numbers grew rather than diminished - a huge encouragement to our elderly members. And so it was that we tried to encourage an environment of change and Tim would often preach from the front that, "It takes unselfish people to grow a church ". Our elderly ladies were very gracious and although some of the changes weren't things they felt comfortable with or got excited by, they nonetheless allowed us to introduce new things and slowly, one by one, new people started to come through the doors on a Sunday morning. Sometime later as the church continued to grow, Tim went to visit one of those original old ladies in hospital just before she died and her first question was, "How many people were in church on Sunday? " When Tim answered her question her eyes grew wide with amazement and she replied, "Where do they all keep coming from? " The answer is, from the prayers of the faithful men and women like her who over many years and decades asked God to bring revival to the little gospel hall and in his goodness God has honoured those prayers with numerical and spiritual growth.

When we inherited the pre-fab building that was the Gospel Hall, we had a grand sum of £400 in the church coffers but the building desperately needed a major overhaul. The roof was full of asbestos so one of the first things we did was to have the church re-roofed. We then systematically knocked down inner walls to make bigger rooms, planned and fitted a new kitchen, levelled out floors throughout the building and laid a solid wood floor, built a new baptistry and fitted glass doors on the front of the building to make it more welcoming and modern. All this was done with the help of grants from Christian organisations plus the generous giving of church members and amazingly everything was paid for. We met in other community buildings in the town on a temporary basis while all this work was going on and then returned to the refurbished Gospel Hall once all the modernisation had been completed. And in his goodness, God added to our numbers. It was if he was saying – "See, I have already begun!

Chapter Twelve

2 Corinthians 4:18 (NLT)
So we don't look at the troubles we can see now; rather, we fix our gaze on things that cannot be seen. For the things we see now will soon be gone, but the things we cannot see will last forever.

Fly

The launch into new territory of Pastoring a church came at a time of great personal struggle for me when my faith was tested as I tried to understand the plans and purposes of God in the lives of those close to me.

We had been very good friends with a young couple in their early twenties, Jodie and Roy, who attended our old church in Newent. Both of them had actually been in Tim's Sunday School class many years previously so it was a long-standing friendship. Jodie and Roy were married one December afternoon in 2000 at Glebe Chapel in a beautiful candlelit service and soon after bought their first house in Steam Mills, Cinderford. Tim and I were very honoured to be the first guests to be invited for a meal to their new home and they seemed very happy together. However, living in the heart of the Forest as newly-weds they felt a bit isolated from friends and family in Newent so made the decision to move back to Newent where both sets of parents lived.

Sometime after this they started hosting a Homegroup in their home primarily for the twenty-something's in church which Tim and I helped co-lead. It was a happy time and our little group enjoyed meeting up each week to encourage one another and to study the Bible together. During this period the four of us enjoyed a holiday together in Cyprus. We shared a two-bedroom apartment and had a wonderful week of eating, swimming in the sea and sight-seeing. Roy made us laugh by having an odd way of eating Weetabix. He would pile three of them up on the table next to his dish then drop one into his bowl, splash some milk on it and gobble it down quickly. The whole process would then be repeated twice more as he didn't like them to be soggy! It made breakfast times very entertaining.

We decided to have a ride on a giant inflatable banana one day pulled behind a speedboat but Jodie lost her nerve at the last minute leaving me wedged between the two men as we took off along the shoreline at great speed bouncing from wave to wave as I shrieked at the top of my voice and practically deafened Tim who was in front. The ride ended by the speedboat doing a sharp turn which then capsized the inflatable banana, tipping the three of us into the sea and forcing us to swim to shore. We have lots of happy memories of that holiday together not least having a fit of the giggles on our balcony one evening when we simply could not get a grip. Every time one of us said something it just started the other three off and we were crying helplessly with laughter and in the end we had to retire back into our apartment as we were getting frosty looks from the people on the neighbouring balcony. It was a special time and we returned home bronzed and relaxed.

Another, albeit less relaxing, holiday we shared was when we went camping in the Lake District for a few days. We borrowed my brother-in-law's six man tent which Tim, being a seasoned camper, assured us he knew how to erect! Having packed all the equipment into the boot of our car we headed off up the M5 to Keswick. We arrived in the late afternoon in a steady drizzle, laid the tent poles out on the grass and stood back to await instructions from Tim on how to assemble the frame. He stood looking at the pile of metal poles with a somewhat perplexed look on his face and finally admitted it had been a while since he had put a tent like this together at which point we all groaned inwardly. However being intrepid explorers, after a few false starts, we eventually had the frame built and the cover on and tied down. We unpacked the contents of the car and soon had a homely feel to our temporary home despite the inclement weather. Jodie and I went off across the field to explore the facilities and later that night saw the four of us crammed into the central sleeping compartment like peas in a pod. Jodie and I slept in the middle with Roy and Tim on the outside but I don't recall sleeping at all that first night as the wind got up and the rain lashed against the canvas. With every gust of wind I was convinced the tent was going to disappear from over our heads and we would be exposed to the elements but Tim and Roy were oblivious to imminent catastrophe as they snored theirs heads off and slept soundly!

We happily explored the delights of the Lake District and as we were driving along the road we saw the white froth of a waterfall up on the side of the mountain and dared Roy to run up to it and back. As always he was up for a challenge and so we pulled over and he leapt from the car and up the steep slope like a mountain goat. We watched him wind his way upwards till he reached his goal, touched it and made the return journey arriving back hot and breathless but pleased to have completed the challenge.

Roy had a dream to be a farmer and to own a farm of his own. His parents had a little bit of land near their house on the edge of Newent and Roy kept a few sheep there. He liked nothing better than to be out on a tractor or pottering around the fields and would offer his services to farming friends to help with milking cows and lambing in the spring. He was also a talented musician and played the cornet in Glebe Chapel band as well as for the A.W.Parker Drybrook Brass Band which he had been a member of since he was eight. Roy also started doing a bit of speaking on the occasional Sunday evening at the church in Newent as the leadership sought to encourage some of the younger men to explore their gifts and try their hand at preaching. Jodie and Roy decided to start a family and their daughter Leah was born in the summer of 2002. All was looking rosy and life was sweet.

At the end of 2003 Roy started feeling unwell. He lost weight and had a lot of pain in his abdomen so eventually after several trips to the doctors, they diagnosed appendicitis. He was taken into hospital and his appendix was removed but the medical staff were surprised that it wasn't inflamed as they had expected. He was sent home but the symptoms persisted and the pain got worse so he had various tests and scans and was diagnosed with cancer of the colon. He was just 22. They operated again to remove the cancerous section of colon and then he underwent a course of chemotherapy and was finally given the all-clear in September 2004. It was around this time that the four of us had a break away for a few days on the Yorkshire Dales. Tim and I rented a cosy little cottage and Jodie and Roy came to join us as they had been up north for a wedding. We did day trips out to Haworth where the Bronte sisters hailed from and also to see the cottage thought to have inspired "Wuthering Heights ". Roy was still weak from the chemotherapy and so opted to stay at the cottage some of the time but we enjoyed ourselves and had fun.

At the beginning of 2005 Tim's cousin made the decision to sell his dairy farm. Roy had been doing quite a lot of the milking for him and so this would have an obvious impact on him and it started him thinking about pursuing his dream of being a farmer. He knew he wasn't in a position to buy a farm outright but decided to explore the option of being a tenant farmer. He filled in the necessary paperwork for a tenancy that was coming available for a small farm in Sandhurst, Gloucester and waited to see what happened. Much to his delight he was offered the tenancy. Not long after this I recorded the following in my journal:

> 23rd February 2005
> Lord, I bring Jodie and Roy to you today and ask for your hand of blessing to be on them. Roy went back into hospital yesterday morning because he was in a lot of pain and has got a hard lump in his stomach. Please Lord don't let it be cancer again. He's been through so much already. Lord, they've only just got the offer of a farm and a new venture - please don't snatch it away from them now. I pray you'll give Jodie a sense of your peace and help her to stay positive - it

must be like a recurring nightmare. Please give the doctors and consultants' wisdom and skill as they diagnose the problem and I pray your hand will be in everything that's done. Please draw near and be all that they need for comfort, strength and guidance at this time.

For the next week or so Roy underwent various tests and had a biopsy and it was just a matter of waiting. The diagnosis was not good. The cancer had returned and was terminal. My journal reads:

7th March 2005
Thank you for a lovely time at Roy and Jodie's last night - it was good just to sit and chat and laugh together. Thank you for the gift of friendship that we share - it seems all the more precious now that we may not be able to enjoy Roy's company for much longer. Thank you that our friendship is eternal, that it spans time and the constraints of this earth and that we'll still be able to enjoy each other's company in heaven. Please draw especially near to Jodie, Roy and Leah over the next weeks and months. Pour your love, peace and joy into their hearts and may they feel the reassurance of your presence watching over them.

It felt like we were being pulled in all directions. There was excitement and anticipation over the new work starting in Cinderford and the imminent arrival of the Bible School students who were coming to spend their placement with us but at the same time there was a dark cloud hanging over us as we saw Roy's health deteriorate. In my journal entries over this period my emotions yo-yoed continually. I was angry at God for letting this happen then the next moment I was contrite and asking God to perform a miracle and heal Roy or to be merciful and call him home. I felt useless as I watched Jodie hold it all together and nurse Roy at home as well as continue to keep everything as near to normal as possible for their daughter Leah's sake. She was utterly amazing. We continued to meet up each Sunday evening at their home but occasionally Roy was too tired as the cancer took its toll.

23rd March
I pray for Jodie and Roy today. I saw Jodie yesterday and she looked so tired and world-weary. Roy's now got a drip for the morphine and even that wasn't keeping the pain at bay. He hadn't slept for the last two nights. Lord, I can't imagine what it must be like to watch someone you love suffer so much pain. It must be tearing Jodie apart. Please Lord, be merciful and don't make him suffer any more. Please release him from this world and take him home to be with you. Lord, Jodie's probably terrified of being left alone so please draw nearer than you have ever been to her and wrap your loving arms around her. Please Lord absorb her fear, her pain, and her sadness and replace it with your deep peace and quiet strength. Be everything that both of them need right now.

Just over a week later my oscillating emotions had me praying for his healing.

3rd April
I've just been reading about the impact of overcoming faith and it made me think of Roy. Today is the day on which he was meant to be giving his testimony of how he trusted you when he was diagnosed with cancer the first time around. Now he's dying Lord and his body is a shell of what it used to be - ravaged by cancer which has come back with such a vengeance. I still believe Lord that you can say the word and he will be healed. I know you have the power to step in and restore him back to full strength and health but maybe your plan is to let him pass through death's door to have maximum impact. I don't know your mind Lord, I can't see the bigger picture - I just know that it hurts to see someone you love go through such pain but then I don't need to tell you that, you already know. Lord, what bigger impact could

there be than you healing Roy this morning? Then he could walk into Chapel and give his testimony - people would see how emaciated he is and know that the only explanation is the healing power of the Sovereign God. How can his death have more impact than that? Lord, I don't mean to question your plans but I pray now that you might intervene and touch Roy right now as he lies in his bed - just stoop down from heaven and breathe your healing into his broken and hurting body. Tell him he's got to go to Chapel to share the good news with those there so what he's been through will have maximum impact and your great name will be glorified. Please Lord hear and answer me - I know you can! Please give him another chance to do your work here on Earth, to be so full of your grace that it touches many people's lives. May this close brush with death help him to re-evaluate his life and may it impress upon him the importance of putting you first. Lord, I don't know what else to pray - everything else seems to pale into insignificance compared to this huge request - I'm expectant. Amen.

There was no miraculous intervention and a week later on 10th April, our 12th Wedding Anniversary, Roy died. My journal entry that day reads:

I must admit when Tim told me it was like a big weight had been lifted off me and at the moment I don't feel sad. If anything I feel a happiness and a light-heartedness when I think of what Roy is enjoying right now. He's in the very presence of his God, the one who has held his hand all through life, who has guided his steps and has finally welcomed him home. Lord, I can't even begin to imagine what joy he is experiencing right now, what unfathomable truths are being revealed to him, what surprises are awaiting him. Please help Jodie and the rest of the family to catch hold of that thought, to look at death through Roy's eyes and to know the peace that comes from the assurance that he's safely home, wrapped in the loving arms of his Heavenly Father. Lord, draw near. Stoop down from heaven and gently touch their hurting hearts with your love.

The funeral took place six days later and was a wonderful celebration of Roy's short but full life. The brass band he had been a member of for so many years were invited to play and Tim and I were honoured and touched to be asked to take part too. Tim gave a tribute and I read a poem I had written for Roy during those final weeks of his life. We still keep a holiday snap of the four of us in Cyprus on the side in our bedroom in which we all look bronzed and relaxed. Jodie and Roy gave it to us on our return home in a lovely wooden frame and the Bible verse inscribed on it is Proverbs 17:17, "A friend loves at all times, and a brother is born for adversity. " Little did we know then of the adversity that lay in wait on the road ahead but they walked the path set before them with courage and dignity and only when I get to heaven will I fully understand what God was achieving in the midst of their struggle.

FLY

The battle's won so have no fear
For while death's form may hover near –
There is no need to run and hide,
For Jesus stands there at your side.
At his command dark shadows flee
And heaven's distant shore you'll see –
Your pain and tears things of the past
As on His face you gaze at last.
The joy you've known here on the earth
Will pale compared to Heaven's mirth;
Such wonder, beauty, love and grace
Reflected in the Father's face.
So say goodbye and loose your hold
To go where streets are paved with gold,
No backward glance, no longing sigh –
Just spread your wings and heavenward fly.

Chapter Thirteen

Matthew 14:27-28 (NLT)
But Jesus spoke to them at once. “Don’t be afraid, “ he said. “Take courage. I am here! “
Then Peter called to him, “Lord, if it’s really you, tell me to come to you, walking on the water. “

Walking on Water

As anticipated I didn't find the transition from being a farmer's wife to a pastor's wife an easy one. It seemed to me that overnight people had a different expectation of me, that I was now the fount of all knowledge and people looked to me to take a lead in various situations. Up until now I had been safely huddled in the boat but now I was being called to walk on water and it was a frightening experience. Unlike Peter who had requested that Jesus call to him to give him the courage to step out of the boat, I felt like I was having my fingers prized off the side of the boat and being pushed into uncharted, shark infested waters completely against my will.

At the beginning of 2005 we spent a few months visiting other churches and quietly implementing small changes whilst still operating under the name Station Street Chapel. One of the first things we did was to change from a 3pm afternoon service to a morning service and on 5th June we saw 41 people come through the doors. As a result of that first morning service one young woman recommitted her life to Christ and a young man felt convicted to ask for baptism so it was a huge encouragement. The weeks and months passed in a blur of busyness as we prepared for our official launch as The Forest of Dean Community Church in March the following year. As well as running a B&B business I was now involved in helping with the Mother & Toddler group, leading a small Bible Study group, teaching Sunday School each week and having people around for meals to our home in order to get to know them better. As the pace of the B&B business picked up over the summer period life got even more hectic and in my journal for 30th August 2005 I wrote:

> "Lord I feel frazzled. I feel like I'm stood on the brink of an abyss and one little push will send me over the edge. Lord, I just love coming to you because I can be me. I don't have to put on a false smile and make out that everything's fine. I don't have to say the right things so that you'll think well of me. I can come and let all my defences down - let you see the unadorned me, the little girl who doesn't have all the answers, who is tired of always being there for everyone else, who is running on empty yet who is still expected to keep on giving. Lord, you don't ask anything of me. You just let me be. Thank you. Thank you for understanding. Thank you for being my bolt hole, my refuge, my hiding place. Thank you for the luxury of allowing me just to be. I think sometimes Lord that you're my sanity. When things get too much and I feel like I'm being pushed nearer the edge, I come to you for restoration. "

During this season in my life as I made the transition to being a pastor's wife I often poured out my heart to God. Tim was busy with casting a vision for the new church, preaching each Sunday and strategizing for how the church might grow and so I didn't feel I could dump all my struggles and worries on him. Instead I took them to God. With God I knew I could be completely open and candid - there was no point trying to pull the wool over his eyes as he knew me better than I knew myself. I don't find it easy to express my emotions and in all the years we have been married Tim has rarely seen me cry but God has frequently had a sobbing wreck on his hands when things overwhelm me. I valiantly tried to juggle all the balls without dropping any of them for many months but things didn't get better and so a year later, one afternoon in August 2006 I wrote the following letter to Tim:

20th August 2006

Dear Tim,
As you know I have always found it easier to say things in writing rather than face to face and so I've decided to explain how I've been feeling lately although it's difficult to know where to start.

I guess the long and short of it is that I'm not happy. I feel harassed and pressurized and I feel like I've got to wear a false smile and be someone I'm not. I thought it was just a passing phase, that I'd snap out of it but I'm feeling the same way now as I was this time last year so it's not just going to go away like I had hoped.

When you felt called to be a pastor I didn't have that same calling but I assumed that if God was calling you to Cinderford then he must want me to be part of it too and so he would equip me for the job. I was wrong. He hasn't given me a heart for the work like you and I resent it if I'm honest.

You have four days a week to prepare your sermon, organise your Homegroup material, visit people and generally look after the smooth running of the church. I don't. I still have a full time business to run, shopping to buy, meals to prepare, washing to do, the house to keep clean and friends and family to keep in touch with (although I'm not doing very well at that!). In addition I now have a Sunday School lesson to plan, Homegroups to organise and church members to visit. In September there will be Koffee & Kids again and also the Coffee Lounge to fit in on a weekly basis. You have a day off when you can have a lie-in but I've often got B&B guests to feed and rooms to get ready for new ones arriving before we can go off and do anything for the day. I just feel constantly harassed and then you want me to entertain and have people back for meals which at one time I would have loved doing but now it's just one more thing putting pressure on me and weighing me down. I just feel tearful all the time and it's not like me. I know I'm moody and short with you and I'm aware I'm being horrible but I don't know how else to deal with it. Sometimes I just want to pack my bags and leave so no-one will find me but I know that's stupid and totally impractical. Nonetheless it's how I feel. It's as though everyone wants a piece of me and because I'm the pastor's wife I have to be all smiley and be there for everyone and meet their expectations. I can do it on the outside but inside I'm cracking up and sometimes I have the urge to shout and yell all sorts of terrible expletives which would shock everyone (me included) because I feel so angry. Last summer you were sat out on the decking reading a book on our day off and I was hanging out the washing on the line with tears streaming down my face because I was feeling so low. I was praying to God to give me a sign that he understood and all of a sudden a little robin landed in the tree right by the washing line and started to sing the most beautiful song. He wasn't scared of me, he just sat there and sang his heart out. It was just what I needed – a gift from God to lift my spirits as he acknowledged my despair. I stopped crying and felt a real peace as if God was saying, "Hang on in there, it will get better! " But it hasn't. A year later I still feel low and God hasn't sent me another robin to cheer me up.

I guess a lot of my anger is directed at you. You seem to think I'm super woman and can handle everything and you make comments when I turn down bookings and say I'm not a businesswoman. To be honest, I'm not making a very good pastor's wife either. Often I don't want to talk to people and I don't want to talk about church. I just feel that God has made a big mistake. You're right for the role and I'm not and it's making me unhappy trying to be someone and something I'm not. It's like trying to put a square peg in a round hole – it doesn't fit! When you start talking to people about church related things I just think, "Here we go again! " which isn't how a pastor's wife should be feeling. Then I start feeling guilty that I don't share your passion but it doesn't make me any more enthusiastic. I resent Kidszone too. Just because I was a teacher doesn't mean to say I still want to teach. I've moved on from that part of my life. I know it's not your fault and that there is no-one else to do it and that it's an area that I need to serve in right now even if it's not my primary ministry but you don't help by making your talks so long. You're doing what you enjoy and so you make the most of it – I'm doing what I struggle with and it's prolonging the agony!

I'm sorry to go on and to be so negative. I've battled with this for over a year now and I kept putting off saying anything to you because you've had enough on your plate with all the pressures you're under. It's been a steep learning curve for both of us but you seem to be happy and flourishing in your new role and I feel like a fake. As time goes on I feel angrier and more stressed and I don't know how to reverse the trend. I don't expect you to have the answers but I just wanted you to be aware of what's going on in my head and why I behave the way I do sometimes. I'm sure it's the devil trying to get at me but knowing that doesn't make it any easier – he's still very persistent! God is probably growing me – I just wish it wasn't such a painful process.

I guess I'm just trying to say don't push me too hard and just give me some space when I'm feeling frazzled. I don't find it easy to talk about things because I don't want to break down and cry – only God has that privilege! The good thing is that I still feel close to God. I doubt his wisdom in the role he's given me but we're on good speaking terms and he's taken the brunt of my anger and frustration when I've been mad at you. You should be grateful that he's such a good shield!

Love,
Nina x x x

I left the letter on the bed and went out to run the Youth Group for the evening, hoping Tim would find it and read it while I was gone. He did and was worried about me as he hadn't realised how badly I was struggling. When I returned home later that evening we sat down and talked as he tried to help me find a way of reducing my commitments, thereby easing the pressure I was under. We made just two simple changes which helped enormously. Firstly, I stepped back from being involved in the Mother and Toddler group which I never felt was my forte as I don't relate to toddlers and have never been a mother so have no wealth of experience to draw upon or share with others. Secondly, I found someone else to help me teach the Kidszone Sunday School class so that I was able to do it fortnightly instead of every week. Probably what had an even greater impact than these two changes was the fact that I had been listened to. I had voiced my struggles and Tim had heard my cry for help and validated me. He had proved he wasn't just there as a pastor for those in the church but had shown that as my husband he loved me and cherished me and that my wellbeing was of huge consequence to him. Church leadership is about teamwork and supporting one another. I had learned some important lessons. People can't mind-read and unless I tell them how I'm feeling how will they know? Also, I learnt the importance of listening to and validating others when they share their hearts with me.

I would like to say that the incident described here was a pivotal moment from which point I never looked back but that isn't the case. I still find at times that my schedule is frenetic, that people's expectations are high, that I'm doing my juggling act again and I'm in danger of dropping the balls. However, one day in my quiet time I came across this verse in Isaiah that challenged me and resonated with me and has been a favourite verse since;

Isaiah 30:15 (NLT)
This is what the Sovereign LORD,
the Holy One of Israel, says:
"Only in returning to me
and resting in me will you be saved.
In quietness and confidence is your strength.
But you would have none of it."

I have to choose to return to God and seek his face in the midst of busy periods. I have to find time to sit with him and to be quiet before him for it is then that he strengthens me and equips me for the fray. Usually the first thing to go out of the window in busy spells is my quiet time but this is when I need to have that time alone with God the most and it is something I am trying to learn, albeit slowly and repeatedly.

SOLACE
When life gets tough and the road's uphill
When loved ones' expectations are a bitter pill,
When tiredness has seeped into your core
And you feel like you can't go on anymore.
When all you want is to close your eyes
As the panic you're quelling begins to rise,
You feel you can't cope with what's ahead
And fear of failure fills your mind with dark dread.
When those you love appear not to care
About the feelings you're so desperate to share,
Then turn to the one whose nail-pierced hands
Will lovingly lift you and help you to stand
Against the storms that life brings your way
By giving you the strength to face each new day.

Looking back from the vantage point of ten years on down the line, I can see that my struggles were indeed growing pains. God needed to stretch me, to challenge me, to rub off sharp corners and teach me patience. He showed me I couldn't do it alone – I needed others to walk with me through the storms. He taught me to be real and not pretend. He showed me that making myself vulnerable was a good thing as it encouraged others to do the same. However, I don't always get it right.

Just recently a good friend said something to me that at first horrified me but then on reflection, I could see the truth of her words. She had been going through a particularly turbulent few years in her marriage and had poured out her heart to a few close friends who had attempted to support her through a tough season in her life. One day, after the storm had passed, she and I were chatting together and she said, "Sometimes you need friends that comfort you and sometimes you need friends to give you a kick up the back side. You are the friend I know who will listen but not pity. You will give me the kick I need as you won't let me wallow in self-pity. You have a way of making me pull myself together, and get on with life. " If I'm honest a little part of me was hurt to be told this was her perception of me but when I thought about it, I could see the truth of her observations. God, in his wisdom, has made us all unique. We are all different and have different personality traits which in turn means we relate to others in differing ways. Some people are gentle and supportive, they hand out the tissues and make soothing noises when someone is having a crisis. Others are less emotional, can see past the tears to what action needs to be taken as their minds weigh up the various options. I think I fall into the latter category. That's not to say I am immune to others' anguish. I have been reduced to tears on many occasions by other people's pain and hurts but I tend not to show it while I am with them - I reserve that for when I converse with God on their behalf later.

The other attribute I have learnt is a life-saver in this role is a thick skin and for this I owe my thanks to my dad. As my sister and I were growing up, my dad loved to tease us and would say all kinds of things that would scar some people for life or at the very least give them a complex but I was secure in the knowledge that my dad loved me and was only playing. I have always had quite solid legs and dad used to call them "hearts of oak, " and make other such disparaging comments about my physical appearance! Anyway, the long and short of it is, it takes a lot to upset me! I have had people phone me to apologise for things they have said which might have hurt me when I have been totally unaware of the perceived snub. This has been invaluable as a pastor's wife as it helps me not to take myself too seriously and I soon came to the conclusion that it is impossible to please everybody all of the time. In fact I love the quote from Os Guinness in which he says, "I live before the audience of One - before others I have nothing to gain, nothing to lose, nothing to prove. " We will never succeed in keeping everyone happy all of the time so we should focus our energy on living lives that please God. He is the only one whose approval we should seek and whose good opinion we should desire.

Tim has often said to me you need a tough skin and a soft heart to be a leader and he's right. If your skin is too soft you will get constantly bruised and punctured by hurtful words which can then fester and steal your joy. I didn't know it then, but my dad's teasing and playful jibes were a training ground for me and were a means of producing the thick skin I needed for the role as pastor's wife so I am very much indebted to him. I love you dad.

At this point in my narrative perhaps I should explain how I feel now about being a Pastor's wife.

Despite my initial reluctance to step into the role and the internal battles I waged with myself and with God, I can say that I have since found a sense of deep fulfilment and joy. It has been challenging to be dragged out of my comfort zone but I have learnt a great deal about myself and other people in the process and I have learnt a much deeper dependency on God. There have been countless "firsts " as I have taken part in Mission Trips to far flung places like Peru, the Philippines and Rwanda and have had opportunities to share Biblical truths with women and children. I have prayed for dozens of people as they have dedicated their lives to Christ for the first time, spoken in a women's prison, spent two months volunteering in the Garden Tomb in Jerusalem, shared my experiences at coffee mornings and women's meetings and started up a Street Pastor team in the town – all as a direct result of taking that initial step of obedience to be involved in the church in Cinderford.

I sometimes look around at the faces of our church family on a Sunday morning and wonder at the fact that ten years ago I didn't know any of them (with the exception of 2 people) and yet now they are an integral part of my life. We have a large number of people with special educational needs who have taught me to love unconditionally and to be accepting of everyone. We have an inspiring and talented group of young people who encourage me hugely as I see them growing in their faith and impacting the world around them. I have found friendship, love and acceptance in my ladies' Bible Study group as we experience life's journey together with all its ups and downs. I can honestly say that I thank God for the privilege of being involved in peoples' lives as I see him at work restoring, growing, healing and transforming. He is making a pathway through the wilderness of the Forest of Dean and it is an honour to be part of that process and I'm excited to see what the rest of the journey will reveal!

Chapter Fourteen

Psalm 23 (NLT)
The LORD is my shepherd;
I have all that I need.
He lets me rest in green meadows;
he leads me beside peaceful streams.
He renews my strength.

Holy Cakes

One of the privileges of being a pastor's wife is that I have the opportunity to get involved in people's lives. One such person I want to tell you about here gave me renewed enthusiasm for my prayer life and reminded me of the amazing power and grace of the God I serve.

In August 2007 Tim and I found ourselves in the Tower Block of Gloucester Royal Hospital going to visit a man we had never met before but about whom we had heard a lot of stories. Slim was the husband of Lin who had been a regular attender of our church and he had been diagnosed with pancreatic cancer. He and Lin were devastated because he had already survived a bout of chemotherapy for cancer of the colon a few years previously and had been given the all-clear 12 months earlier. Slim didn't 'do God' and whilst he never stopped Lin from coming to church it certainly wasn't anything he felt had any relevance for him and so it was with trepidation (mainly on Lin's part!) that we had arranged to go and visit him. Slim was a man's man, a car mechanic, who had lived a colourful past and his language had a tendency to be somewhat colourful too so all in all Lin was all of a twitch as we walked into the ward on that summer's afternoon. However, despite her misgivings, we got on like a house on fire and because one of Slim's past jobs had been an animal food delivery driver, he and Tim had plenty to talk about and the time flew by.

That was the first of many afternoons spent with Slim. He was then referred to Queen Elizabeth Hospital in Birmingham for an operation in which they hoped to cut away the cancerous tissue and we went to visit him there too. Unfortunately the cancer had spread too far and so surgery to remove it was not an option. He was devastated. He was offered a chemotherapy course which he started as soon as he had recovered from the surgery. Lin was warned that the cancer was terminal and treatment would only prolong his life, not cure him. So began our weekly Tuesday visits to Lin's kitchen in Cinderford where Slim would sit in 'his corner' by the table and we would talk about holidays, friends, work, past experiences and the goings-on at church. Each week I would take home-baked cakes which Slim would hide from their eldest son, Billy, who nick-named them 'Holy cakes' because they had been baked by the vicar's wife! On one occasion both Lin & Slim came over to the farm for lunch and Slim was keen to go and see the milking and look around the farm and it was a really happy day.

As the months went by we could see a gradual deterioration in Slim. When we went on a mission trip to the Philippines in December that year, I made him a DVD in which I read some of my Christmas poems by our log burner and introduced him on film to a little calf I had been looking after and which I had been telling him all about on our Tuesday afternoon visits. When we got back from our trip Lin said he had watched it and she had seen a little tear trickle down his face – this man's man wasn't so tough after all. The months passed and Slim's weight began to plummet – in just one week the change was dramatic. He slept more and everything was an effort. Our weekly visits continued but the home-baked treats were no longer hoarded away in his corner and Billy ended up being the consumer of the holy cakes. We continued to talk about church and the effect God had on people's lives and Slim would drift in and out of the conversation. Lin was desperate to see Slim become a Christian, saying that it was more important than him being healed. She understood that his eternal destination was of greater importance than a few more years of life no matter how appealing that might be. As her church family we felt it was important to have a day of prayer and fasting for Slim's salvation as we sensed the end was fast approaching. On Thursday 26th June 2008 everyone who felt able to, put a day aside to do just that. I bought a Dictaphone and on that day I walked around the fields near our farm and talked to Slim like I had never talked to him before. I told him that God loved him no matter how many bad things he had done in his life. I described the Holman Hunt picture of Christ knocking at the door and spoke of Revelation 3 vs 20. I told him God had been knocking at his heart's door for 60 years – didn't he think it was time to let him in? I begged, I pleaded, I laughed, I cried – if anyone had seen or heard me they would have thought I had completely lost the plot and I thought Slim would probably come to the same conclusion when he listened to the recording. It didn't matter. I sensed God was giving him one last chance and I prayed with all my heart. The next day I gave the recording to Lin to pass on to Slim.

The following Monday lunch time the phone rang and I answered it to hear Lin's voice on the other end of the line, sobbing her heart out. My immediate thought was that we had been too late – Slim had died. After a few moments of unintelligible gabbling I realised I had jumped to the wrong conclusion – Slim was still in the land of the living. The reason for Lin's tears was that just moments before, in the kitchen we had sat in so many times, Slim had asked Lin to pray with him and help him commit his life to the Lord. She was ecstatic – her longed for miracle had happened and God in his grace had allowed her to be the one to lead her husband to the Lord. We sat on either end of the phone and cried together. I will never forget that moment and will count it as one of the greatest bitter-sweet moments of my life.

For the next 23 days before his death Lin and Slim prayed together every morning and evening – something Lin would never have imagined possible in her wildest dreams. On one occasion when Lin got carried away and prayed for longer than usual, Slim interrupted and told her to keep it short because God had a lot of other people's prayers to listen to and he didn't think they should have the monopoly! He also loved her to read Psalm 23 to him which she did most days and neither Lin nor I can sing that song now without thinking of him. The day before he died Tim and I went to visit Slim who was heavily sedated with morphine. As we left I took his hand and kissed him and he held on tight and looked me intently in the eye. I think he was saying goodbye.

On the day he died, Lin phoned us and asked us to go around to the house. When we arrived it was as it had always been – full of people and noise. We sat among their friends and family and listened as they reminisced on stories and events in Slim's life. It was an honour to be allowed to be close to a family's heart at such a poignant time. Andrew, their youngest son, was on tea-making duty and brought both Tim and me a mug of tea so I was rather taken aback when seconds later Lin whisked Tim's mug out of his hand and disappeared into the kitchen muttering something about it having a crack in it. It turned out that Andrew had inadvertently given Tim one of Slim's mugs with a rather dubious caption on it saying in large letters, "Two nuts ", and underneath in small print, "A massive spanner ". Lin explained afterwards that as Andrew had headed in Tim's direction with the offending mug she had come over all peculiar, rapidly thinking how she could alleviate the situation and the only excuse she could think of was to say that the mug had a crack. A confused Andrew followed his mum back into the kitchen where his brother Billy took one look at Lin's mortified expression and asked what was wrong. Lin pointed to the ambiguous caption on the mug which spurred Billy on into daring her to take it back out and give it to Tim for a laugh. After some persuasion she finally agreed to do this at the same time as asking for forgiveness for telling a lie. Tim was bemused by the whole thing and had been totally oblivious to the mug's caption but Lin's obvious discomfort gave everyone else a laugh!

The funeral took place at the Baptist Church in town as we knew it would be well attended and our little Gospel Hall would not be big enough. The service was at 10am and half an hour before this there was a queue of mourners all along the road waiting to get in despite the fact that the undertaker had omitted to announce the funeral in the local paper. Afterwards we discovered there were more than 500 people (mainly men) at the funeral who filled the Baptist Church for the first time in many years. Tim took the service and as he stood up to speak he felt as though a wall of hostility had been erected as if people were holding invisible hands over their ears, determined not to hear the message. He said he has never before or since felt such a strong almost tangible negative force. Thankfully, as he prayed for God's help and strength, God brought to mind a story we had heard on the night of Slim's death with regards to his mother-in-law. The tale was told that Lin and Slim were going out for the night and Slim's mother-in-law had agreed to babysit for them. They lived in a 2 bedroomed cottage and so decided that as it would be very late when they got home from the party, the mother-in-law would sleep upstairs in their bedroom and they would sleep downstairs on a mattress in the lounge. When they got home from the party late that night rather the worse for wear, Slim had to visit the bathroom upstairs and in his befuddlement completely forgot about their arrangement. He came out the bathroom, ripped all his clothes off and jumped into bed completely naked with .... his mother-in-law! As Tim related this story, everyone laughed and the barriers they had erected suddenly came crashing down as they realised that this minister did know Slim and had earnt the right to speak at his funeral. I was able to read a poem I had written which I hoped had captured something of Slim's larger than life character but at the same time spoke of the decision he had made at the eleventh hour:

FOR SLIM
We met in Gloucester Royal one warm summer's afternoon –
Poor Lin was like a cat on bricks in the corner of the room!
She wanted us to meet you but was scared of what you'd say
Her worries were unfounded for you were well behaved that day!

We got on like a house on fire talking about the past
And the time spent by your bedside seemed to rattle by so fast;
That was the first of many times we'd come and chat with you
In the corner of your kitchen as we sat and had a brew.
Each Tuesday afternoon I'd bring you home-baked cakes to try
You'd hide them in your corner away from Billy's searching eye!
We got to know you week by week as the stories would unfold,
And soon discovered when God made you, he threw away the mould!
We'd sometimes find you working in your garage out the back
And your vast knowledge of car engine parts never seemed to lack!
I learnt a new vocabulary sitting there with you
And no, I don't mean swear words, for of those there were very few!
You talked about past holidays – your love of France and Spain
And hoped that you'd be well enough to visit there again;
But God had different plans though as he whispered in your ear
Inviting you to let Him in so He could take away your fear.
You had fought that still, small voice all your life since a young lad,
Thinking that you weren't good enough, that your life had been too bad;
But Slim you were so peaceful on the day you let God in
And when you made that choice there was no one happier than Lin.
You see many have been praying that you would understand
How God has prepared a place for you in a bright and distant land;
How He wanted you to know Him, to feel his Father's love
And I know we'll meet again one day, in heaven up above.

God used Slim to teach me a lot. He reminded me that He is big enough to soften the hardest heart. He showed me that there is no better way to share our faith than to walk alongside people and be real. He reminded me of the importance of persistent prayer even when things look hopeless. I thank God for letting my path cross with Slim's and no doubt Slim would be bemused to think he had been instrumental in my Christian growth. The amazing thing is that Lin and Slim's youngest son, Andrew, is now quite a regular attender at our church events with his wife and three children. In fact, Hannah, the oldest grandchild, has just been baptised this month (August 2015) and her testimony as an eight year-old was very powerful. Slim died just before the second grandchild Thomas was born and then Daniel came along some years later. I'm sure it would put a smile on Slim's face to see the three of them coming along to church week by week – God's work isn't finished yet!

Chapter Fifteen

1 Peter 1:17 (NLT)
And remember that the heavenly Father to whom you pray has no favourites. He will judge or reward you according to what you do. So you must live in reverent fear of him during your time here as "temporary residents."

Homesick

As I write this final chapter we, as a church, are starting a period of 40 days asking the question "What on Earth am I here for? " It is such a big question. The simple answer is that we are here because God made us so that he could lavish his love on us. How amazing is that? And another astounding fact is that God planted eternity in our hearts (Ephesians 3:11) so that those who love him get to be with him forever.

I don't know about you, but I sometimes feel world weary. I listen to the news, read the newspapers, see the mess, the pain, the selfishness and the hopelessness in the lives of people around me and long to be free of it. I find myself telling God often that whenever he sees fit to call me home, he won't find me putting up a fight - I'm ready to shuffle off this mortal coil and claim my new heavenly body. Then I begin to feel guilty. What about the family and friends I'll leave behind? What about those who don't know Jesus yet? What about those people so desperately clinging on to life while I'm so quick to relinquish it?

These thoughts are expressed in the following poem I wrote many years ago:

HOMESICK
Lord, I feel a longing deep down in my soul
To fill this aching emptiness
And by you to be made whole.
I'm weary of this race, the endless road ahead;
Of being in this hurting world
Where countless tears are shed.
I'm tired of temptations whichever way I turn,
Time and time again I fall,
I never seem to learn.
You tell me this is not my home,
That I'm just passing through
I'm tired of being a foreigner,
I want to be with you.
I long to gaze upon your face,
To worship at your throne,
I yearn to be held in your arms
As I am welcomed home.
But Lord, I find myself still here,
No matter how I plead -
So grant me grace to do your work
Of sowing precious seed;
That through my strivings here on earth,
I may earn a golden crown,
And on the day you call me home,
At your feet I'll lay it down.

I guess it's all about priorities. Paul wrote in Philippians 1:21 (NLT) "For to me, living means living for Christ, and dying is even better. " As Christians we shouldn't hold on to life here on earth too tightly because we're just passing through, we're temporary residents and our real home is in heaven. However, we have been called to be the aroma of Christ, to be salt and light in a world that badly needs it and so while God sees fit to leave us here, we should spend our time and energy in trying to be just that.

I struggle with the fact that my Dad and my sister see no need for God in their lives and it breaks my heart. I can't even begin to imagine an eternity without them and no doubt many reading this book can identify with me as you think of friends and family members who are in the same boat. I have tried to share my faith with them on numerous occasions. I have written letters to them both pleading for them to explore the truth of God's love and grace but to no avail. If I allow myself to dwell on it I find myself being dragged down into the depths of depression and hopelessness so I have learnt to step back and simply commit them to God. He is in the saving game - that's not my department! He has called me to live my life in such a way that honours him and brings him glory. If I make that my aim every day (and believe me I slip up frequently!) I can leave the rest to the Holy Spirit. I believe I serve a God who is good and gracious and who is the embodiment of love. I don't need to allow myself to be overwhelmed by the fact that many of my friends and family as yet don't have a relationship with him - I trust that he will work in their hearts and lives in his time and in his way.

On another level, the thought of eternity makes me work at my relationships with fellow Christians now. It's no good me saying I don't get on with someone or don't appreciate some personality trait - the long and short of it is that I will be spending eternity with them so I had better get to like them! I know we will all be made perfect in heaven so there won't be a clash of egos but God uses the here and now as a training ground in which to knock off the prickly, rough edges of our characters. We all tend to think of ourselves as beyond reproof and to see the character flaws in others but isn't there something about removing the plank from our own eye before we attempt to remove the speck from someone else's? Maybe if we're not very good at identifying our weak spots we need to ask a trusted friend to hold us accountable on the understanding we won't get defensive if they criticise some aspect of our behaviour or personality. We need to constantly weed out the negative attitudes that hold us prisoner and allow the fruit of the Holy Spirit to take root instead. This is beautifully conveyed in The Message translation of Galatians 5:22-23,

"But what happens when we live God's way? He brings gifts

into our lives, much the same way that fruit appears in an orchard—things like affection for others, exuberance about life, serenity. We develop a willingness to stick with things, a sense of compassion in the heart, and a conviction that a basic holiness permeates things and people. We find ourselves involved in loyal commitments, not needing to force our way in life, able to marshal and direct our energies wisely. "

I believe that my greatest calling is to be the person God made me to be so I must guard against allowing others to define my shape. I need to remind myself often that I am loved unconditionally - nothing I do will make God love me more or less, I am already fully loved and that love will not be withdrawn if I do something foolish. Many years ago, when I started on this journey of being a pastor's wife, my sister-in-law gave me a little book by Lynne Hybels called, "Nice girls don't change the world ". I have read it time and time again and it speaks truth into my life as Lynne shares her struggle through black depression and into the light beyond. Her astute observations are relevant not only for pastor's wives but for everyone who is seeking to live their lives in the light of God's love. Her battle with depression caused her to step back from everything and to rest, and in that place of quiet solitude God met with her and regenerated her tired soul. God's words embraced her with a gentle love and they are the words that he whispers to each of us today if only we will be still enough and quiet enough to listen:

"I love you, right here, right now. I love you so much I want you to rest. I want you to sit and receive the refreshment of my creation. I want you to listen to music. I want you to dance in the quietness of your bedroom. I want you to be like a child, secure and free in the presence of an adoring parent. I want you to know that for all those years when you were working so hard to try to please me, I was trying to tell you to slow down. I saw you killing yourself from the inside out and I tried to stop you but the many false voices in your head drowned out the single true voice. I wasn't the one cracking the whip, the one telling you to work harder, the one who made you feel guilty when you relaxed. I was the one who saw you, who knew you, who believed in you, who longed to restore your energy. I was the one trying to fluff up the pillow, tuck the blanket around your shoulders, and tell you it was time to rest. I was the one trying to love you. "

I love the imagery of our heavenly Father fluffing up the pillow and tucking us in, of watching over us while we sleep. As time goes by I am becoming more and more aware that I need to strive less and to just 'be' because God isn't impressed with my busyness but rather more by my availability and obedience. The expectations I set for myself or allow others to set for me will eventually cause me to crash and burn but Jesus' words in Matthew 11:28-30 show me a healthy alternative;

"Are you tired? Worn out? Burned out on religion? Come to me. Get away with me and you'll recover your life. I'll show you how to take a real rest. Walk with me and work with me—watch how I do it. Learn the unforced rhythms of grace. I won't lay anything heavy or ill-fitting on you. Keep company with me and you'll learn to live freely and lightly. " God's burden is not heavy or onerous – it is the burdens we place on ourselves that weigh us down.

As I have written this book I have enjoyed revisiting the various memories which had me smiling one moment and then feeling melancholic the next yet the one thing that struck me overwhelmingly as I look back over my life is the faithfulness of God. People have come and gone as my life has meandered through different seasons. There have been ups and downs, times of joy and times of difficulty, times when the choices have been clear and times when they've been shrouded in uncertainty. But underpinning all these things, God has been the constant in my life even when I was unfaithful and for this I am ever thankful. It is this knowledge that makes the future less scary. I know that whatever lies around the corner, good or bad, I will not be walking the road alone because God has promised that he will never forsake me. My calling is to be an instrument that God can use for his glory and I am content to be a tool in the master's hand. This is beautifully depicted in the words of Mother Teresa;

"I am a little pencil in God's hands. He does the thinking. He does the writing. He does everything and sometimes it is really hard because it is a broken pencil and He has to sharpen it a little more."

I just hope he doesn't need to sharpen me too much!

About the Author

Katrina lives with her husband Tim on a dairy farm near Ross-on-Wye. She has been a primary school teacher, a farmer's wife, a B&B proprietor and more recently a pastor's wife. She supports Tim as he pastors the Forest of Dean Community Church in Cinderford (www.fodcc.org) which they planted in 2005. Katrina leads a weekly Bible study group and 'The Core' which is a church youth group. She enjoys walking, reading, listening to music, baking, decorating and doing crosswords.

52486737R00072

Made in the USA
Charleston, SC
20 February 2016